Higher ENGLISH

LANGUAGE SKILLS

for CfE

Mary M. Firth and Andrew G. Ralston

SCOTTISH EXAMINATION MATERIALS

HODDER GIBSON
AN HACHETTE UK COMPANY

The Publishers would like to thank the following for permission to reproduce copyright material:

Photo credits p.34 © The Grassic Gibbon Centre; **p.35** © Claudio Divizia – Fotolia; **p.36** © Ulrich Willmünder – Fotolia; **p.44** © REX; **p.53** © REX; **p.59** © Slaven Vlasic/Getty Images; **p.71** © Stuart C. Wilson/Getty Images.

Chapter opener image reproduced on pages v, 1, 5, 10, 14, 17, 18, 32, 39, 48, 54, 58, 63, 66, 68, 71, 74, 78, 80, 82, 85, 89, 93, 96, 97, 99, 100, 101, 102, 103, 104, 106, 107 and 110 © Rido – Fotolia.com.

Orders: please contact Bookpoint Ltd, 130 Park Drive, Abingdon, Oxon OX14 4SE. Telephone: (44) 01235 827720; Fax: (44) 01235 400454. Lines are open 9:00–5:00, Monday to Saturday, with a 24-hour message answering service. Visit our website at www.hoddereducation.co.uk. Hodder Gibson can be contacted direct on: Tel: 0141 848 1609; Fax: 0141 889 6315; email: hoddergibson@hodder.co.uk

© Mary M Firth, Andrew G Ralston 2015
First published in 2015 by
Hodder Gibson, an imprint of Hodder Education,
An Hachette UK Company,
2a Christie Street
Paisley PA1 1NB

Impression number   5 4 3 2
Year   2019 2018 2017 2016

Cover photo © Rido – Fotolia.com
Illustrations by Barking Dog Art Design and Illustration
Typeset in 12/14.5pt Minion Regular by Integra Software Services Pvt. Ltd., Pondicherry, India
Printed in Spain
A catalogue record for this title is available from the British Library.
ISBN: 978 1 471 83799 9

CONTENTS

INTRODUCTION

You can't revise for the Reading for Understanding, Analysis and Evaluation paper.

Have *you* ever said that?

Obviously, because this part of Higher English is based on 'unseen' passages, you can't revise the content in advance or memorise quotations.

But many students don't realise that questions relating to the content of the passage are only one aspect of the paper. At least as much emphasis is placed by the examiners on the style of language used in the passage. *Such questions are not only asking you about what the writer is saying; they are asking you about how he or she is saying it.*

You *can* revise for these questions by training yourself to recognise the language features that help to make up a good written style.

For some authors, a good style comes naturally…

Thriller writer Edgar Wallace used to sit at his desk and produce 10,000 words a day, keeping up his strength by drinking 30 cups of tea and eating doughnuts. He wrote the screenplay for the film *King Kong* in nine weeks and composed so quickly that it was said that he could turn out a novel in the back of a taxi in a traffic jam.

…while others find it much more difficult:

The nineteenth-century French novelist Gustave Flaubert did not have a natural flair for writing and would spend hours on a single sentence. He rewrote his most famous book, *Madame Bovary*, five times, never looking back at his previous version.

Every professional writer – whether he or she writes quickly and instinctively like Edgar Wallace, or slowly and painstakingly like Gustave Flaubert – has mastered the skills of word choice, sentence structure, tone, imagery, punctuation and so on. If you have never studied these techniques, you will not be able to answer questions on them and will end up making vague guesses. This book will explain the techniques, but it will do something else as well: it will train you to understand what the wording of questions is getting at, and will show you methods for approaching different kinds of questions.

If you work through this book systematically, by the time the Higher examination comes round you will have realised that:

You **can** revise for the Reading for Understanding, Analysis and Evaluation paper!

1 UNDERSTANDING THE MEANING
USING YOUR OWN WORDS

Some close reading questions, like the example below, are designed to test whether you can successfully extract information from a piece of writing and thus demonstrate that you understand what a writer is trying to communicate.

From the first paragraph, identify two…   **(2 marks)**

There are two stages in answering questions of this type:

- **Identify** the words in the passage that contain the answer.

- **Translate** the appropriate expressions into your own words.

Warning!

It is essential that you do not 'lift' whole phrases or sentences from the original: these will not be awarded any marks, *even though you have understood the question and the answer is correct.*

Some tips on using your own words

- You can use simple words from the original passage if there is no obvious alternative. For example, if a common noun such as 'eye' is used, there is no need for a clumsy rephrasing like 'organ of vision'.
- Figures of speech and any non-standard expression such as slang must always be put into plain language. Try to rephrase in a simple but formal style.
- A good approach is to think of *synonyms* – i.e. words that mean the same as a given word. For example, if you were asked to explain the word 'distraught', suitable alternatives would be 'very anxious', 'desperate' or 'distressed'. When you are doing practice exercises in class or at home, use a thesaurus to help with this.
- If you cannot think of a synonym, try thinking of the *opposite* and use this in your answer. For example, as an alternative to 'generous', you could say 'not mean'. This proves to the examiner that you understand what 'generous' means.

What the examiner is looking for…

Every exam paper has a marking scheme, which specifies the number of marks allocated to each answer. A marker will look for the required amount of information before awarding full marks. As you work through the paper, you must take careful note of the marks available for each question

Warning!

A very common error in an exam is to write too much for the first few questions. This may cause you to be short of time and force you to skimp on later questions that are worth more marks. Remember, even if you answer brilliantly, and at length, the marker cannot give you more marks for individual questions than the marking scheme allows.

and proportion your answers accordingly. For example, a question worth 2 marks may require you to identify two pieces of information; a question worth 4 marks will require either four brief pieces of information or two more fully developed ones. It is equally possible to gain the 4 marks by a combination of brief and more fully developed points.

Worked example

The remains of the medieval cathedral of St Andrews rear up at the east end of the town like the bones of a gigantic dinosaur. The outline of the former church dazzles by its sheer extent – it was Scotland's largest in an age of extravagant ecclesiastical building. The guidebook describes the architecture of the ruins and the main artefacts exhibited in the cathedral museum. But it doesn't mention the aura of profound peace to be found within this ancient place of worship.

Question

Identify the two features of St Andrews Cathedral that most struck the writer. **(2 marks)**

Method

Identify the words in the passage that contain the answer.	Translate the appropriate expressions into your own words.
'The outline … dazzles by its sheer extent … Scotland's largest in an age of extravagant ecclesiastical building.'	*The vast extent of the ruins reveals that the original church was exceptionally large.*
'the aura of profound peace to be found within this ancient place of worship.'	*A deeply peaceful atmosphere prevails in the grounds of the cathedral.*

Answer

The writer was most impressed by the vast extent of the ruins, showing the original church had been exceptionally large **(1 mark)**, and by the deeply peaceful atmosphere within the grounds of the cathedral **(1 mark)**.

For practice

Use the same method in the following examples, providing more or less detail as the number of marks suggests. To help you with the first one, the relevant words have been 'identified' for you in the left-hand column of the table. You should now 'translate' them into your own words.

1. Legend has it that Eynhallow, one of Orkney's uninhabited islands, was at one time the hidden Hildaland, a vanishing island that came and went. It was an enchanted isle where blood would flow from stalks of corn if they were cut after sunset. Cats, rats and mice could not live there. At one time soil would be brought from Eynhallow and put under haystacks or new houses to keep vermin away.

(*Source: The Islands of Orkney* by Liv Kjørsvik Schei)

Question

Identify four of the beliefs held about the island of Eynhallow that contributed to its supernatural reputation. **(4 marks)**

Identify the words in the passage that contain the answer.	Translate the appropriate expressions into your own words.
'a vanishing island that came and went.'	
'blood would flow from stalks of corn if they were cut after sunset.'	
'Cats, rats and mice could not live there.'	
'soil would be brought from Eynhallow and put under haystacks or new houses to keep vermin away.'	

2. Myself, my family, my generation, were born in a world of silence; a world of hard work and necessary patience, of backs bent to the ground, hands massaging the crops, of waiting on weather and growth; of villages like ships in the empty landscapes and the long walking distances between them; of white narrow roads, rutted by hooves and cartwheels, innocent of oil or petrol, down which people passed rarely, and almost never for pleasure, and the horse was the fastest thing moving.

(*Source: Cider With Rosie* by Laurie Lee)

Questions

a) Explain the nature of agricultural work during the author's childhood. **(2 marks)**
b) Identify three further aspects of village life at that time. **(3 marks)**

3. When one came straight from England the aspect of Barcelona was something startling and overwhelming. It was the first time that I had ever been in a town where the working class was in the saddle. Practically every building of any size had been seized by the workers and was draped with red flags or with the red-and-black flag of the Anarchists; every wall was scrawled with the hammer and sickle and with the initials of the revolutionary parties; almost every church had been gutted and its images burnt.

(*Source: Homage to Catalonia* by George Orwell)

Question

Identify four reasons why the author found Barcelona astonishing. **(4 marks)**

4. We do not know how art began any more than we know how language started. If we take art to mean such activities as building temples and houses, making pictures and sculptures, or weaving patterns, there is no people in all the world without art. If, on the other hand, we mean by art some kind of beautiful luxury, something to enjoy in museums and exhibitions or something special to use as a precious decoration in the best parlour, we must realise that this use of the word is a very recent development and that many of the greatest builders, painters or sculptors of the past never dreamed of it.

(*Source: The Story of Art* by E.H. Gombrich)

Questions

a) In your own words, identify three types of activities that have always been considered to be 'art'. **(3 marks)**
b) Identify three things that the writer says would only in recent times be considered 'art'. **(3 marks)**

5. The winter of 1542 was marked by tempestuous weather throughout the British Isles: in the north, on the border between Scotland and England, there were heavy snowfalls in December and frost so savage that by January the ships were frozen into the harbour at Newcastle.

    These stark conditions found a bleak parallel in the political climate that then prevailed between the two countries. Scotland as a nation groaned under the humiliation of a recent defeat at English hands at the battle of Solway Moss. As a result of the battle, the Scottish nobility – which had barely recovered from the defeat of Flodden a generation before – was stricken yet again by the deaths of many of their leaders in their prime; of those who survived, many prominent members were prisoners in English hands, while the rest met the experience of defeat by quarrelling among themselves, showing their strongest loyalty to the principle of self-aggrandisement, rather than to the troubled monarchy. The Scottish national Church, although still officially Catholic for the next seventeen years, was already torn between those who wished to reform its manifold abuses from within, and those who wished to follow England's example, by breaking away root and branch from the tree of Rome. The king of this divided country, James V, lay dying with his face to the wall.

(*Source: Mary, Queen of Scots* by Antonia Fraser)

Questions

a) Explain what was noteworthy about the winter of 1542. **(2 marks)**
b) In your own words, identify five political problems that were facing Scotland. **(5 marks)**

LINK QUESTIONS

A type of question that is designed to test your understanding of the *structure* of a text is the so-called link question. You will be asked to show how one sentence provides a 'link' in the argument. The 'argument' need not be a discussion; here 'argument' means the progression of ideas in a piece of writing and the link will join one idea to the next. An example of a link question is:

> 'And therein lies the rub.' Explain how this sentence acts as a link between the first paragraph and the two following paragraphs.
> **(2 marks)**

Usually, but not invariably, the 'link' sentence will stand at the beginning of a paragraph. Part of the sentence – often, but not always, the first part – will refer back to the previous topic and another part of the sentence will introduce the new topic that follows. Such questions are usually worth 2 marks, one of which is awarded for correctly identifying the **two parts of the sentence** that link back and forward, and the other for summarising in your own words the **two topics** that they connect.

A tried and tested method is to show the link by:

- **quoting** the part of the link sentence that refers *back* to the earlier topic
- explaining **in your own words** what this topic is
- **quoting** the part of the link sentence that looks *forward* to the next topic
- explaining **in your own words** what the next topic is.

If the sentence begins with or contains a linking word or phrase you should also comment on this. Expressions such as 'but' and 'however' point to a contrasting idea, or change of direction, while phrases such as 'moreover' or 'in addition' show that the next idea offers further support to the same argument.

The diagram below shows a selection of linking words and phrases.

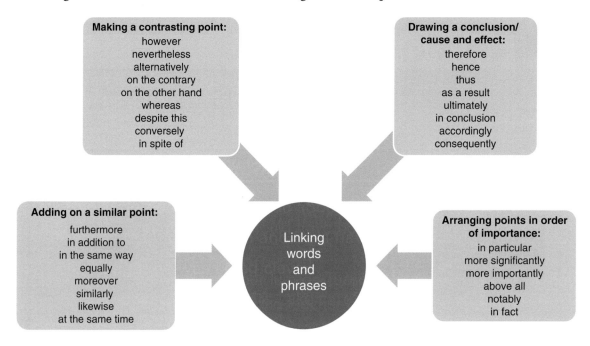

Worked example

William Shakespeare is easily the best known of our English writers. Virtually every man in the street can name some of his plays and his characters, and many people can also recite lines of his poetry by heart.

Despite our familiarity with his work, however, we know relatively little of the man himself. We do not know when or why he became an actor, we know nothing of his life in London, and almost nothing of his personal concerns.

Question

Show how the highlighted sentence acts as a link in the argument.   **(2 marks)**

Answer

- The phrase 'our familiarity with his work' looks back at the topic of how widely known Shakespeare's work is.

- The conjunction 'however' suggests a contrasting idea to follow.

- The second part of the sentence, 'we know relatively little of the man himself', introduces the new topic.

- This deals with what is not known about Shakespeare, and a list of things follows the 'link' sentence.

For practice

1. My mother was born near Gloucester, in the early 1880s. Through her father, John Light, she had some mysterious connection with the castle, half-forgotten, but implying a blood-link somewhere. Indeed, it was said that an ancestor led the murder of Edward II.

   But whatever the illicit grandeurs of her forebears, Mother was born to quite ordinary poverty. When she was about thirteen years old her mother was taken ill, so she had to leave school for good. She had her five young brothers and her father to look after, and there was no one else to help.

   (*Source: Cider With Rosie* by Laurie Lee)

Question

Show how the highlighted sentence acts as a link in the argument.   **(3 marks)**

2. Usually his mother would caution Yang the chauffeur to avoid the old beggar who lay at the end of the drive. This beggar had arrived two months earlier, a bundle of living rags whose only possessions were a frayed paper mat and an empty tobacco tin that he shook at passersby. He never moved from the mat, but ferociously defended his plot outside the gates. Even Boy and Number One Coolie, the houseboy and the chief scullion, had been unable to shift him.

   However, the position had brought the old man little benefit. There were hard times in Shanghai that winter, and after a week-long cold spell he was too tired to raise his tin. After a heavy snowfall one night in early December the snow formed a thick quilt, from which the old man's face emerged like a sleeping child's above an eiderdown. Jim told himself that he never moved because he was warm under the snow.

   (*Source: Empire of the Sun* by J.G. Ballard)

Question

Show how the first sentence of the second paragraph acts as a link in the argument.   **(3 marks)**

3. Mary Stuart was certainly rated a beauty by the standards of her own time: even John Knox described her as 'pleasing'. In her height, her small neat head, and her grace she resembled the contemporary ideal. It was the type of beauty that her contemporaries were already learning to admire in art, and could now appreciate in life, all the more satisfyingly because it was in the person of a princess.

   Not only the appearance, but also the character of Mary Stuart made her admirably suited to be a princess of France in the age in which she lived. Mary was exactly the sort of beautiful woman, not precisely brilliant, but well-educated and charming, who inspired and stimulated poets by her presence to feats of homage.

   (*Source: Mary, Queen of Scots* by Antonia Fraser)

Question

Show how the highlighted sentence acts as a link in the argument.   **(2 marks)**

4. The popular press found copy in Einstein. Newspaper photographers discovered a highly photogenic subject – his was a face of character: drooping, kindly eyes and wrinkles of humour surrounded by a leonine mane of hair. The habits of the man were a little irregular; already some of the characteristics expected of the absent-minded professor were beginning to show: he lived a simple life uncluttered by possessions and any of the outward trappings of success; when there was no need to be careful he was careless about his dress: sometimes he wore no socks.

    All these qualities, combined with the publicised qualities of the man – kindliness, gentleness and warmth – would still not have been sufficient to turn Einstein into the international figure he was to become. The missing ingredient in this recipe for public fame was the apparently incomprehensible nature of Einstein's work. For a few years after the publication of the general theory of relativity only a limited number of scientists familiarised themselves with it in detail. Its abstruse nature became legend and absurd stories sprang up around its esoteric significance. It was even rumoured that there were few men in the world who were capable of understanding the theory.

Question

Demonstrate that the highlighted sentence performs a linking function between the two paragraphs.   **(2 marks)**

5. To us the sheer profusion of servants on the nineteenth-century scene is striking. In 1851 between 7 and 8 per cent of the entire population of the country were servants, if we ignore children under ten. For women and girls the figure was over 13 per cent and for them 'service' was so much the commonest job that it accounted for nearly twice the number employed in the whole textile industry – by far the most important group of manufacturers and one in which the majority of workers was female. It can almost be said that every family that was able to feed and clothe some sort of servant kept one. Within this vast and heterogeneous army conditions varied, from the miserable child-of-all-work sleeping on a sack under the stairs, in bondage for a few coppers a week and her wretched keep, to the great magnate's house steward, a prosperous member of the middle class.

Question

Show how the highlighted phrase relates to what has gone before it and introduces a new idea to be developed in the remainder of the paragraph.   **(2 marks)**

6. At school, Alastair had shown exceptional promise. He had excelled as a scholar, as a musician and on the games field; his popularity and talent had made him an obvious choice for head boy in his last year.

His university career made a sad contrast to the years as a golden boy. A baffling lack of commitment saw him fail his first year exams, and after a nervous breakdown early in his second year he dropped out altogether.

Question

Show how the highlighted sentence acts as a link.   **(2 marks)**

DENOTATION AND CONNOTATION

At Higher level you will be expected to show a more sophisticated awareness of the meanings of words than has been previously required. In addition to understanding the *denotation* of a word (the literal definition of a word as given in a dictionary), you will also be expected to fully appreciate its *connotations* – the ideas it is associated with. These connotations determine whether the word has a *negative* or *positive* impact, and affect the *mood* and *tone* a writer intends to convey.

> George Orwell chose to use pigs to exemplify human vices in *Animal Farm* because of their negative connotations.

For example, the *denotation* of the word 'pig' is simply a farm animal, but it has many negative *connotations*, such as dirtiness, greed and laziness. Similarly, the dictionary definition of 'swarm' is 'a group of bees or other insects moving together', but when applied metaphorically 'swarm' implies an unpleasantly large and invasive group. The word '**pejorative**' is used to refer to a negative association like this.

If a word is a metaphor, then it will have the connotations of the original denotation to enhance the meaning. For example, if a team of young gymnasts is said to be 'well drilled' it implies an intensive training similar to soldiers being 'drilled'. This could create a **critical** tone, as overly harsh military discipline would seem inappropriate for teaching sport to children.

For practice

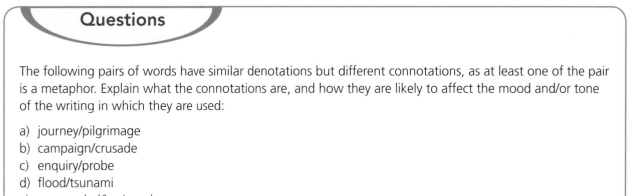

Questions

The following pairs of words have similar denotations but different connotations, as at least one of the pair is a metaphor. Explain what the connotations are, and how they are likely to affect the mood and/or tone of the writing in which they are used:

a) journey/pilgrimage
b) campaign/crusade
c) enquiry/probe
d) flood/tsunami
e) surrounded/besieged.

SHADES OF MEANING

Connotations may not always be so clear cut as when metaphors are used. A **thesaurus** gives lists of synonyms – if you consult a dictionary you may find it gives a similar definition for many of them. On reflection, however, you may feel the words are not identical, but have significant shades of meaning. We associate certain words with certain contexts, which influences our understanding of them.

Positive/negative connotations

If you look up the word 'confident' in a dictionary, you will find the word 'bold' given as a definition. Although these words are similar, however, they have different associations. 'Confident' is more representative of a person's inner self, whereas 'bold' tends to reflect how a person responds to external situations. While 'confident' is usually **positive** in connotation, 'bold' can sometimes be negative. We would approve of a 'confident' child, but for a child to be called 'bold' would have unpleasant connotations of impudence.

On the other hand, for someone to make 'a bold move' in business would imply approval of a daring, clever and perhaps unexpected act, while the expression 'a confident move' would have less impact, merely suggesting the person expected to be successful. Thus, while 'confident' and 'bold' are similar in meaning, the context is important in deciding the shade of meaning each word will have.

For practice

Questions

1. There are numerous words connected with the idea of liveliness. Here is a selection of ten of them.
   a) Put a tick in the correct column according to whether you think the word has a positive or negative effect.
   b) Comment on any particular connotations you associate with each word.

   The first one has been done for you.

	Positive	Negative	Might be positive *or* negative	What you associate with the word
vigorous	✔			Often used to describe plants that grow well.
dynamic				
rumbustious				
rowdy				
unruly				
boisterous				
wild				
hyperactive				
lively				
energetic				

2. Explain the shades of meaning between the following pairs of words. The first has been done for you.
   a) childlike/childish
      Answer: *Both words relate to behaving in a way associated with a very young person. 'Childlike' means 'like a child' and has generally neutral or slightly positive connotations of innocence. 'Childish' has negative connotations as it suggests the person is acting in an immature manner.*
   b) inquisitive/nosy
   c) question/interrogate
   d) shrewd/calculating
   e) gloomy/sullen

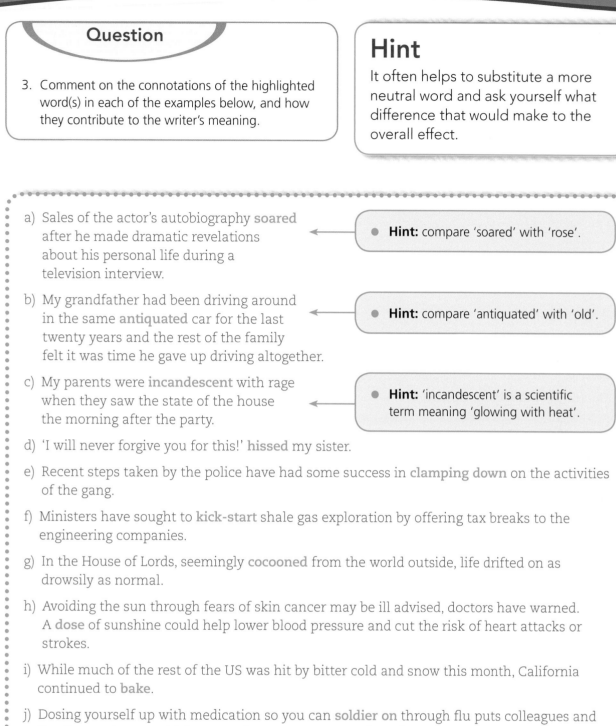

Question

3. Comment on the connotations of the highlighted word(s) in each of the examples below, and how they contribute to the writer's meaning.

Hint

It often helps to substitute a more neutral word and ask yourself what difference that would make to the overall effect.

a) Sales of the actor's autobiography **soared** after he made dramatic revelations about his personal life during a television interview.

→ ● **Hint:** compare 'soared' with 'rose'.

b) My grandfather had been driving around in the same **antiquated** car for the last twenty years and the rest of the family felt it was time he gave up driving altogether.

→ ● **Hint:** compare 'antiquated' with 'old'.

c) My parents were **incandescent** with rage when they saw the state of the house the morning after the party.

→ ● **Hint:** 'incandescent' is a scientific term meaning 'glowing with heat'.

d) 'I will never forgive you for this!' **hissed** my sister.

e) Recent steps taken by the police have had some success in **clamping down** on the activities of the gang.

f) Ministers have sought to **kick-start** shale gas exploration by offering tax breaks to the engineering companies.

g) In the House of Lords, seemingly **cocooned** from the world outside, life drifted on as drowsily as normal.

h) Avoiding the sun through fears of skin cancer may be ill advised, doctors have warned. A **dose** of sunshine could help lower blood pressure and cut the risk of heart attacks or strokes.

i) While much of the rest of the US was hit by bitter cold and snow this month, California continued to **bake**.

j) Dosing yourself up with medication so you can **soldier on** through flu puts colleagues and family members at risk because drugs to suppress a fever increase the amount of virus in the body.

SUMMARISING THE MAIN POINTS

A typical Higher passage for Understanding and Analysis will put forward a point of view and present evidence to support it. Some of the questions are likely to ask you to state one or more of the main points the writer is making, and the final question will ask you to compare the arguments in two passages.

Example

Look at this extract from a newspaper article on the subject of biofuels.

> Biofuels – derived from food crops including corn, sugar cane, palm oil and oilseed rape – are one of the few technologies with the potential to displace oil as a fuel for transport and are seen as a way to cut greenhouse gas emissions.
>
> (*Source:* Jessica Aldred, *Guardian*)

This could be summarised as follows:

Biofuels have the potential to replace oil as a fuel for transport, and to cut greenhouse gases.

Detailed explanations and evidence should be omitted. It is not essential to use your own words at all times, but doing so may help you state the point more briefly.

For practice

Question

The two extracts that follow are from the same article. Summarise the main point(s) made in each paragraph.

(2 marks)

> a) Biofuels have a number of benefits, which include being carbon neutral (that is, the carbon they emit in the atmosphere when burned is offset by the carbon that plants absorb from the atmosphere while growing), renewable (fresh supplies can be grown as needed), secure in their supply and able to be cultivated in many different environments.
>
> b) While biofuels are potentially an important part of the future, any assessment of their merits must be weighed against a number of factors. Firstly, each biofuel must be assessed on its own merits. The term biofuel covers a wide variety of products with many different characteristics and a wide range of potential savings in terms of greenhouse gas emissions, the report said. Secondly, each assessment must address the environmental and economic aspects of the complete cycle – from the growth of the plant to its end use and potential for pollution. Such assessments would help to determine the extent to which different biofuels are carbon neutral, the report said.
>
> (*Source:* Jessica Aldred, *Guardian*)

Question

Summarise the three objections to biofuels put forward by the writer in the following extract.
(It is acceptable to bullet-point your answers.)   **(3 marks)**

In almost all aspects, biofuels are a disaster. Current EU biofuels take up an area of European farmland larger than the size of Belgium, and a similar area is used internationally for European imports. The biofuel farmland in Europe uses as much water as the rivers Seine and Elbe combined.

Moreover, farmers use fast-growing trees like poplar, willow and eucalyptus for biofuels. Unfortunately, these trees emit a chemical called isoprene, an air pollutant that can affect human health. A study by Lancaster University shows that increasing the crop yields to meet the EU's 10 per cent target will increase air pollution, cause an extra 1400 deaths, and cost £5.2 billion annually.

But most important, in moral terms, is the fact that using land to grow fuel rather than food is an abomination in a world where almost a billion people still go hungry. It is estimated that European biofuels now take up enough land to feed 100 million people, and the United States' programme takes up even more.

(*Source:* Bjørn Lomborg, *Daily Telegraph*)

Question

Read the newspaper article below. The table following it summarises the main point of each paragraph. Match up each of the short summaries in the table with the number of the paragraph to which it relates. The first two have been done for you.

Our daughters can become whatever they want

1   More than 200 girls queued outside Hammersmith Town Hall last Friday morning. Aged 10 and 11, they were to sit an entrance exam for one of the best local state secondaries. In the bitter cold, I shivered beside my daughter and scoured the young faces, with their braces, wide eyes, pert noses – and an unmistakable expression of fear.

2   I wouldn't want to be in their shoes, I thought. These girls have so much pressure – and not just in terms of exams. They're expected to manage a social life that includes online relationships, sexting and selfies; they feel the pressure of a size zero figure; oh, and they must have a career, too.

3   No wonder that a third of young women between 16 and 30 admit to feeling isolated, neurotic and less happy than their mothers. A poll out today shows that self-harm and eating disorders are common, as is a sense of despair.

4   These grim findings seem extraordinary given the progress women have made. Plenty of role models show girls that they can be anything they want to be. So why the defeatism? The high-fliers, unwittingly, may hold a clue. These exceptional women enjoy glittering careers; they're skilled and ambitious. Their example inspires many younger women to follow suit.

→

5   But it is also used as a stick with which to beat the rest. The establishment, made up of career men and women, requires everyone to fit into that mould. As they are the ones who comment and consult, draw up policy and review laws, they set the agenda. A young woman who has a job as a hairdresser, say, quickly learns that by making do with a job in the low-skilled sector, she has let down the side. The establishment finds her guilty of sticking to the pink-collar ghetto, where salaries and standards are low.

6   The same applies to the young woman who gets pregnant and decides to stay at home to raise her child. She, too, learns that her priorities disqualify her in the eyes of those at the top – and will result in the government punishing, through taxes, her lack of professional ambition.

7   The hairdresser may love her job, drawing pleasure from transforming the grey and droopy mother-of-three into a Cheryl Cole lookalike. She may enjoy her job's flexible hours and the people with whom it brings her in touch. The mother who opts to stay at home may adore her child and truly believe that her time spent raising the future generation is more important than any career of which she could dream. But both women will learn that decision-makers don't regard their choices as valid.

8   The establishment believes that young girls, given half a chance (or a better education, more benefits, or a home of her own) would choose to be the head of the FTSE. Maybe some would. But many others wouldn't. Their opinions, though, are not broadcast on *Woman's Hour*, featured in the newspapers or sought by the policy-makers. The silent majority must stand by as the elite trashes their lifestyle.

9   I worry for our daughters. They feel forced to conform to the ambitions that a handful of superwomen have for themselves and their 'sisters'. Failure to comply earns the contempt of those who matter. That's hard to bear for a young girl. Surely, women who want to help their daughters should be telling them, 'You can be anything you want – and, yes, that includes a hairdresser, or a stay-at-home mother.'

(*Source:* Cristina Odone, *Daily Telegraph* (condensed))

Main point	Paragraph
Anecdote about the writer's daughter sitting an entrance exam.	1
Girls today face many different kinds of pressure.	2
There are many examples of high-achieving women acting as role models for girls.	
Women should be free to choose the role in life that suits them best.	
Young women today are likely to be more dissatisfied with their lives than those of the previous generation.	
Women who work in lower-skilled jobs or who stay at home may find their lifestyle satisfying.	
Not all young women aspire to reaching the top of the business world.	
Successful people think that women who choose a domestic role lack ambition.	
High-achievers expect everyone to share similar ambitions.	

II ANALYSING THE STYLE
LANGUAGE CHOICE

Section I looked at questions that test your ability to extract information from a piece of writing and demonstrate that you understand what a writer is trying to communicate.

This section focuses on questions that ask you to analyse the effect of the writer's choice of language.

Such questions are likely to follow the following template:

> **By referring to at least two features of language**, analyse how the writer...

You should refer in your answer to such features as:

- sentence structure
- word choice
- imagery
- contrast
- tone.

(Remember, it is acceptable to answer in bullet-point form.)

SENTENCE STRUCTURE

Many candidates find it difficult to discuss sentence structure. Most end up trying to explain *what the sentence means*, but the task is to analyse *how the sentence is put together*.

Few write as an architect builds, drawing up a plan beforehand and thinking it out down to the smallest details. Most write as they play dominoes: their sentences are linked together as dominoes are, one by one, in part deliberately, in part by chance.

(*Source: Essays and Aphorisms* by Arthur Schopenhauer)

Examiners choose passages that have been carefully crafted by authors who take the 'architect' rather than the 'domino player' approach. To discuss sentence structure successfully you will need to be able to recognise:

- different types of sentences
- how the component parts of a sentence are separated by different kinds of punctuation
- how the component parts of a sentence can be arranged according to various patterns
- how writers use different sentence structures to achieve effects of style.

Different types of sentence

A sentence is a group of words that contains a verb and makes complete sense. It will be one of the following types, each of which has a particular purpose. Understanding these purposes will be helpful in answering questions about the 'effectiveness' of a writer's sentence structure.

Sentence type	Example	Purpose
Statement	Scotland's population is around five and a quarter million.	Statements are usually used in narrative or factual writing to convey information. They end with a full stop.
Question	Is Scotland's population likely to increase significantly in the next ten years?	Questions may be used in reflective or emotive writing. They are frequently used as a **link** in an argument. They end with a question mark.
Rhetorical question	Are we going to sit back and allow our precious green space to be built over?	A **rhetorical question** is a question to which no answer is really expected or to which the answer is obvious; it may have the effect of a strong statement.
Exclamation	What nonsense!	Exclamations are used to convey a **tone** of amazement, shock or strong emotion. Usually, but not invariably, they end with an exclamation mark.
Command	Read and observe the introductory information and safety warnings before using your appliance.	Commands are used in instructions and in writing aiming to persuade, such as advertisements. Commands end with a full stop.
Minor sentence (A number of minor sentences is sometimes called 'note form'.)	He looked in his rear-view mirror. Nothing coming.	In a minor sentence the verb is omitted; usually this is a form of the verb 'to be'. A minor sentence may take the form of a statement, question or command. In this example the verb 'was' is omitted in the second sentence. The words 'Nothing coming' do make complete sense; they are more than just a phrase. It is a more concise and dramatic way of saying 'Nothing was coming'. Minor sentences are used for various reasons: to create impact, suspense or urgency, to suggest informality and as abbreviations in notes and diaries.

Paragraphing

Paragraphing is used to break writing into more easily digestible pieces. You may have noticed that in the past writers often expected their readers to cope with longer paragraphs than do writers of today.

A new paragraph is used to mark the next stage in a narrative or argument. Paragraphing may also be used to achieve a particular effect.

- When a writer wishes a piece of writing to have instant impact, or to be particularly easy to understand, he or she uses very **short paragraphs**. Examples of this might be advertisements, writing for children or articles for tabloid newspapers.

- A short paragraph may be used as a link between parts of an argument.

- A single-sentence paragraph may throw emphasis on to a statement or idea.

- A single-sentence paragraph may be used to slow the action and create suspense.

When you see an unusually short paragraph, you must consider what effect the author is aiming at.

For practice

Question

Comment on the types of sentences used in the following pieces of writing. If the paragraphing is noteworthy in any way, say briefly what is special about it. Then discuss what effects the writers are aiming at.

1. Not since the day I was persuaded by a hairdresser to dye my hair with industrial bleach has my appearance on the streets turned so many heads. Only this time there are slack-jawed looks of admiration rather than mirth.

    I can see the words forming: 'That's the new Jag!' – as I slide by in a ship so white it could outdazzle Liberace's teeth.

    But what of performance? When a car looks this good, does it matter? Of course, it must, or we'd all be wheeling around on Rollerblades and Armani jump suits.

    Well, the news is good. Supreme looks are matched by exquisitely refined mechanics.

    Ah, the new Jaguar. Travelling in style, guvnor.

    (*Source:* Dominic Ryan, *The Herald* (adapted))

2. Jim Margolies had jumped from here. Or a sudden gust had taken him: that was the less plausible, but more easily digested, alternative. His widow had stated her belief that he'd been 'walking, just walking', and had lost his footing in the dark. But this raised unanswerable questions. What would take him from his bed in the middle of the night? If he had worries, why did he need to think them out at the top of Salisbury Crags, several miles from his home? He lived in The Grange, in what had been his wife's parents' house. It was raining that night, yet he didn't take the car. Would a desperate man notice he was getting soaked…?

    (*Source: Dead Souls* by Ian Rankin)

3. TUDOR COTTAGE Furniture SALE

    Want it? Just have it! Enjoy cosy cottage comfort for less.

    PAY NOTHING NOW and ENJOY INTEREST FREE CREDIT!

    Come to our biggest sale ever and treat yourself! Take advantage of fabulous savings on all our luxury sofas and chairs, smart dining and bedroom sets plus our new, bigger-than-ever range of stylish accessories. Amaze family and friends with a brand new look for your home this summer – at bargain prices!

    CLICK tudorcottagefurniture.co.uk, VISIT our showrooms or CALL free on 0800 3 113 113.

4. Shivering, Connie turned out the light in her bedroom. And in the upstairs hall. Downstairs, she turned out the light in the living room, went quickly to the front door and bolted it. She was leaving it when she thought to fumble her way across the room and make sure that the window was locked. It was. If the lights had been seen across the bay… She hastened desperately to turn out the rest. The dining room. Lights out. The windows were locked. The pantry. It was dark. Whimpering, she was afraid to enter it. She flashed on the light to make sure of the window.

    The window was broken.

    (*Source:* 'Uneasy Homecoming' by Will F. Jenkins)

➡

5. If you're interested in the RAF, do pay a visit to 602 Squadron museum. You'll be fascinated by this evocative tribute to a famous squadron. A visit takes the form of a tour led by a true enthusiast – so be prepared for an hour or so discussing the many pieces of memorabilia and old photographs on display; each picture tells a story and every item belonged to someone of note. Look out for the Battle of Britain tie and the book containing the names of men who took part in this famous battle – it is kept open on the page that shows the signatures of the survivors.

    Open: Wednesdays and Fridays, 19:30–21:30 (closed July and August).

(*Source: Glasgow for Free* by Shipley and Peplow)

6. Wednesday 15 February: Unexpected surprise. Was just leaving the flat for work when noticed there was a pink envelope on the table – obviously a late Valentine – which said, 'To the Dusky Beauty.' For a moment I was excited, imagining it was for me and suddenly seeing myself as a dark, mysterious object of desire to men out in the street. Then I remembered Vanessa and her slinky dark bob. Humph.

    9 p.m.: Just got back and card is still here. 10 p.m.: Still there.

    11 p.m.: Unbelievable. The card is still there. Maybe Vanessa hasn't got back yet.

(*Source: Bridget Jones's Diary* by Helen Fielding)

7. The Prime Minister was meant to be giving a speech about helping small businesses by cutting the excessive red tape of business regulation. But he was late. Five minutes passed. Then ten. We sat in silence, waiting. Oh dear. What had happened?

    Perhaps he had got caught up in red tape. All tangled round his ankles and calves, making it impossible to move. A monstrous crimson vine, snaking up his thighs, tightening and tightening. Remorseless. His circulation cut off. Face turning purple. Wheezing, gasping. Hands flailing. Fighting for life.

    Then he bounded on stage, looking hale and hearty, and sailed into his speech. It was all fine. The room sighed in relief.

(*Source:* Michael Deacon, *Daily Telegraph*)

Punctuation

The punctuation used in the extracts above will have helped you to identify which sentences were statements, questions, exclamations, commands or minor sentences. Your understanding of punctuation will not be tested by direct questioning such as 'Why is a colon used here?' You are more likely to be asked to 'Comment on the effectiveness of the sentence structure'. Identifying the punctuation marks used can be a useful way of approaching such questions.

Inverted commas

Inverted commas are used for four main purposes:

1. To indicate the title of a play, book, television programme, etc. (Alternatively, **italics** might be used for this purpose.)

    'Macbeth', 'Sunset Song', 'EastEnders'

2. For spoken words:

    'Is there anybody there?' said the Traveller.

3. For quotations:

   As George Orwell said, 'All animals are equal, but some are more equal than others.'

4. To mark off an individual word or phrase from the rest of the sentence.
   This might be done if a word from a foreign language is used:

   While Americans living in Japan are invariably treated courteously, they always remain 'gaijin' – people from outside.

   (Alternatively, **italics** might be used for this purpose.)

Inverted commas can also indicate that the author wants us to recognise that he is distancing himself from the use of a certain term that might be commonly used but which he does not necessarily agree with. For example:

In Victorian times, foreign travel was the preserve of the 'superior' classes of society.

Here, the effect of the inverted commas is to mock the conceited attitude of those Victorians who could afford foreign travel. It is rather like using the words 'so called'.

Colons, semi-colons and dashes

- A **colon** introduces a quotation, a list, or an explanation, expansion or rephrasing of the previous statement.

- A **semi-colon** is generally a 'finishing' pause, marking the end of a sentence but less firmly than a full stop does. It often comes between two statements that are closely connected, or which balance or contrast with one another. It may also be used to separate a list of phrases.

- A **single dash** can be used to introduce an extra piece of information just as a colon does. It can also be used to indicate a breaking off in a sentence (the technical name for this is '**aposiopesis**'). For example,

  'If we should fail –'

- **Two dashes** can mark off an extra piece of information in the middle of a sentence – a technique known as **parenthesis**. This piece of information can be omitted without affecting the basic structure of the sentence. A writer might use this technique to insert a comment, perhaps to create a humorous or ironic tone:

  After lone male newsreaders had read the news for decades, the powers-that-be decided we needed two people reading the nine o'clock news, and the other would have to be – you've guessed it – a beautiful woman.

- A parenthesis (the plural is parentheses) can also be marked by a pair of commas or a pair of brackets – see below.

- **Hyphen**: do not confuse the dash with the **hyphen**, which when printed is only half the length of a dash. The only use of a hyphen is to link words to produce a compound word, e.g. 'must-have'. Sometimes a writer will create new words ('**coinages**') by hyphenating familiar words – look at the first worked example on page 23 for this usage.

Commas, stops and brackets

- **Commas** are used to separate different grammatical elements of a sentence, such as phrases, clauses, or items in a list. Two commas may mark off a parenthesis, and in this use are often regarded as more formal than dashes or brackets.

- An **exclamation mark** is used to end an exclamation or to suggest a loud voice in direct speech. It is frequently used as an indicator of **tone**, to convey surprise, humour, irony and the like.

- An **ellipsis** (…) is represented by a row of three full stops. It indicates that a word (or words) is left out or implied. Various effects can be created depending on the context: suspense, humour, irony, innuendo, etc.

- A pair of **brackets** may be used to mark a parenthesis, in the same way as a pair of dashes.

Worked examples

Look at the following two examples and the commentaries on the effectiveness of the punctuation used in them.

Example 1

At this time pass all the characters of the Spanish streets: the dark veiled women hurrying home from the priest; the Civil Guard whom nobody greets; gold-skinned sailors and strutting carters; goat-faced ruffians down from the hills; and old men with the hollow eyes of hermits – their skin stretched thin on chill, ascetic bones.

(*Source: As I Walked Out One Midsummer Morning* by Laurie Lee)

- The **colon** in the first line indicates that a list of the 'characters of the Spanish streets' is to follow. Each phrase describing a character or group of characters is separated from the others by a **semi-colon**. If the list of characters had been made up of single words rather than phrases, the writer might simply have used commas:

  women, Civil Guards, sailors, carters, ruffians and old men.

- The writer has also used **hyphens** to coin new words: 'gold-skinned' and 'goat-faced', which help make the description vivid.

- The **dash** in front of the words 'their skin stretched thin on chill, ascetic bones' shows that the author decided to add on a parenthesis, an extra piece of description to reinforce the effect of 'hollow eyes'. ('Ascetic' means austere, spartan, self-denying.) The sentence structure is effective as the list emphasises how varied the different types of people were.

Example 2

There was a king with a large jaw and a queen with a plain face, on the throne of England; there was a king with a large jaw and a queen with a fair face, on the throne of France.

A **semi-colon** is used in conjunction with repetition to create a balanced sentence (a technique known as **antithesis**, which will be explained on page 26). The semi-colon comes exactly in the middle and emphasises the similarity between the occupants of the English and French thrones. The balance and repetition also serve to draw the reader's attention to the one difference between the respective monarchies, however – the queen of France was 'fair' rather than 'plain'.

For practice

Question

Discuss the purpose of the punctuation marks in these extracts.

1. Further on were stalls of slightly better-class goods: plaster dogs, single boots, oil-lamps, singing birds, flowers and gramophones with horns.

2. By some casual mistake of book-keeping the sentence was never carried out; he was abandoned in jail and forgotten.

3. Inside the Cathedral a splendid parade of priests, bishops, choirs, soldiers and city fathers moved to the high altar. The place was full; the singing poor.

(*Source: extracts 1–3 from As I Walked Out One Midsummer Morning by Laurie Lee*)

4. The small translucent bodies of the tiny, crab-like spiders were coloured to match the flowers they inhabited: pink, ivory, wine-red or buttery-yellow. On the rose-stems, ladybirds moved like newly painted toys; ladybirds pale red with large black spots; ladybirds apple-red with brown spots; ladybirds orange with grey-and-black freckles.

5. As soon as we saw it, we wanted to live there – it was as though the villa had been standing there waiting for our arrival.

6. I got to my feet and shouldered my bags and nets; the dogs got to their feet, shook themselves, and yawned.

7. If I found something that interested me – an ant's nest, a caterpillar on a leaf, a spider wrapping up a fly in swaddling clothes of silk – Roger sat down and waited until I had finished examining it.

(*Source: extracts 4–7 from My Family and Other Animals by Gerald Durrell*)

8. Steep rocky red mountains overhung the stream; great oaks and chestnuts grew upon the slopes or in stony terraces; here and there was a red field of millet or a few apple trees studded with red apples; and the road passed hard by two black hamlets, one with an old castle atop to please the heart of the tourist.

(*Source: Travels with a Donkey in the Cevennes by R.L. Stevenson*)

9. It always seemed dark, grey and cold, as if winter had already started, but we did not mind – it was so exciting – so many marvels to see, even the shows outside were wonders – people dancing and 'tumbling' – the pictures of the fat woman, in evening dress, too, and we loved to watch the gold figures on the show-fronts beating their drums and triangles, supposedly in time to the band; they never were.

(*Source: Oil Paint and Grease Paint by Dame Laura Knight*)

10. The old women peered up at me with red-rimmed, clouded eyes, and each tale they told was different: my ex-boss, the hotel-keeper, had been shot as a red spy; he had died of pneumonia in prison; he had escaped to France. Young Paco, the blond dynamiter of enemy tanks, was still a local fisherman – you could run into him at any time; no, he had blown himself up; he had married and gone to Majorca.

(*Source: As I Walked Out One Midsummer Morning by Laurie Lee*)

Question

In the following passage, the writer uses an example of parenthesis (marked by a pair of dashes) in each paragraph. Can you identify what her purpose is in each example?

My parents' generation regarded going out to a restaurant as a wild extravagance: a once-a-year-on-your-wedding-anniversary treat. Restaurants were hushed cathedrals of etiquette, with waiters gliding silently around the room as if on castors. For my generation, by contrast, eating out is something that all but the very poorest take for granted. A government study in 2012 found that Britons spent £180 billion on food, of which £78.1 billion – almost half! – was in restaurants, cafes and canteens.

That figure encompasses a huge range of experiences, of course, from necking a kebab in the street, to sampling the tasting menu at Petrus. The real democratisation of restaurants has – fittingly – happened from the bottom up. Cheap chains such as Pizza Express and Burger King gave the British an affordable taste for eating out.

Traditional restaurateurs, noticing that these new establishments were offering something they lacked – namely fun – have gradually learned to let their hair down. These days, you are more likely to be deafened by the cheerful racket of fellow diners than intimidated into silence.

(*Source:* Jemima Lewis, *Daily Telegraph*)

Sentence patterns

Punctuation is not the only method of structuring sentences. Many sentences depend for their effect on the order in which their component parts are placed.

Hint

Remember the 'two Ps' when thinking of possible answers to sentence structure questions: **punctuation** and **pattern**.

Inversion

In English, the normal order is for the subject to come first, followed by the words that tell us more about the subject (known grammatically as the predicate, which includes the verb). For example,

The flames leapt up and up.

Occasionally, however, this order is reversed:

Up and up leapt the flames.

Here the subject ('the flames') comes *after* the predicate. This technique, whereby the subject is delayed, is known as **inversion** and can be used to alter the emphasis in a sentence.

In his poem 'Church Going', Philip Larkin recalls pausing in a journey to visit a rather dull church with the words, 'Yet stop I did'. The use of inversion is more striking than the normal word order would be ('Yet I did stop'), as emphasis is thrown on to the word 'did'. This conveys more effectively that his action was unexpected.

Inversion tends to be used in shorter sentences in order to stress a particular word. In longer sentences, however, there are several other methods a writer can employ to create emphasis.

Repetition

A writer (or speaker) may decide to repeat certain word patterns for **rhetorical** (i.e. crowd-arousing) effect. During the Second World War, Prime Minister Winston Churchill broadcast many speeches on the radio. One of the techniques he used very skilfully was repetition, as in the famous speech delivered after the evacuation of Dunkirk in 1940:

We shall fight on the beaches, we shall fight on the landing grounds, we shall fight in the fields and in the streets, we shall fight in the hills. We shall never surrender.

(*Source:* Winston Churchill, 4 June 1940)

The series of statements repeating 'we shall fight…' is effective in inspiring his listeners never to give up on their efforts.

Lists, climax and anti-climax

Authors often use the technique of a **list** to present ideas. Whenever you notice a list, you will also usually observe some sort of **progression** in the ideas. A closer look at Churchill's sentence above shows that there is a deliberate order to the places listed. The speaker is tracing the progress of the troops from landing on the beaches, through the countryside, to the towns and to the higher ground beyond, and saying that they would meet with resistance at every stage. The whole list builds up to the last sentence, which has greater impact because it is so short: 'We shall never surrender'. Placing a number of items in ascending order like this, with the most important being kept to the last, is called **climax**.

The opposite effect – when the author builds up to something that does *not* in fact come – is called **anti-climax**.

She crept downstairs, taking infinite care to avoid the loose steps that she knew would creak. Her fingers trembled as they felt for the light switch. Slowly, she pushed open the door, not knowing what to expect. The room was empty.

Antithesis

Another way of arranging ideas within a sentence is to balance opposites together to create a contrast, a technique called **antithesis**. In the poem 'An Irish Airman Foresees His Death' by W.B. Yeats, the pilot wonders why he is taking part in the war:

Those that I fight I do not hate

Those that I guard I do not love.

Antithesis is particularly suited to poetry because its effect can be reinforced by the rhythm, as in the example from Yeats' poem. But the technique is often used in prose as well. Journalists trying to persuade their readers and politicians delivering speeches often use antithesis to state a point in a memorable way. Possibly the politician hopes that journalists will find his comment 'quotable' so that it will find its way into the next day's news headlines. Towards the end of his 1961 Inauguration Address, President John F. Kennedy said:

My fellow Americans, ask not what your country can do for you; ask what you can do for your country.

(*Source:* John F. Kennedy, 20 January 1961)

Kennedy was aiming to make an impressive and statesman-like impact here, but antithesis can equally well have a humorous effect. Scottish comedian Robbie Coltrane published an account of his travels across America in a 1950s convertible, entitled *Coltrane in a Cadillac*. After talking to the owner of a gun shop in Dodge City, Kansas, he observed that:

You can take the American out of the OK Corral, but you can't take the OK Corral out of the American.

(*Source: Coltrane in a Cadillac* by Robbie Coltrane)

Look out for other versions of this popular application of antithesis – you will find it frequently in newspaper articles.

Long and short sentences

We have looked at how the techniques of repetition, climax and antithesis can be used within single sentences. Similar effects can also be obtained with a series of sentences in a paragraph. A piece of writing in which all the sentences are of a similar length or follow the same grammatical pattern will be dull and lifeless to read. A good writer knows instinctively when to balance a long sentence with a short one. Sometimes a short sentence has the effect of an **aphorism**, a pithy saying. This style is described as '**aphoristic**' and is very typical of a minor sentence, such as 'Short but sweet'.

Example 1

In this extract from a short story called 'The Followers' by the Welsh poet Dylan Thomas, different sentence lengths are used to speed up and slow down the narrative:

We ran up the gravel drive, and around the corner of the house, and into the avenue and out on to St Augustus Crescent. The rain roared down to drown the town. There we stopped for breath. We did not speak or look at each other. Then we walked through the rain. At Victoria Corner, we stopped again.

(*Source:* 'The Followers' by Dylan Thomas)

The first sentence conveys a feeling of speed and continuous movement by using the **conjunction** 'and' three times. This contrasts effectively with the short statement 'There we stopped for breath.' The slower, out-of-breath progress of the characters in the rest of the paragraph is conveyed by a series of short sentences.

Example 2

In the following descriptive passage from E.M. Forster's novel *A Room with a View*, the author alternates between short and long sentences:

Miss Bartlett not favouring the scheme, they walked up the hill in a silence which was only broken by the rector naming some fern. On the summit they paused. The sky had grown wilder since he stood there last hour, giving to the land a tragic greatness that is rare in Surrey. Grey clouds were charging across tissues of white, which stretched and shredded and tore slowly, until through their final layers there gleamed a hint of the disappearing blue. Summer was retreating.

(*Source: A Room with a View* by E.M. Forster)

For discussion

Why do you think Forster has placed the two statements 'On the summit they paused' and 'Summer was retreating' as separate short sentences on their own? Try re-reading the passage as if it were punctuated differently and observe whether the description becomes less effective.

What the examiner is looking for

You should now be able to:

- identify different types of sentences
- understand how punctuation is used to clarify the structure
- recognise techniques such as inversion, repetition, climax and antithesis
- observe why authors use varied sentence lengths.

> ## Remember
>
> It is not enough to explain in general terms how a sentence structure feature works; your answer must refer specifically to how it works **in the context of the passage** you are examining.

Worked example

Look at this extract from a past Higher English practice paper that dealt with the subject of the Darien Scheme, an attempt by Scots in the seventeenth century to set up a colony in a remote piece of land in Central America.

> Darien is an isolated finger of land on the northern coast of Panama. Even its climate is awful. The rainy season is relentless, sometimes lasting from April to January; and it is always swelteringly hot. It is inhabited by a primitive tribe and forgotten – quite rightly – by the rest of the world. Except Scotland.
>
> (*Source*: SQA)

Question

Comment on the effectiveness of any feature of sentence structure in reinforcing the writer's opinion.

(2 marks)

Task

For discussion

How good do you think the answers in the table on page 29 are?

Decide (individually or in groups) whether they are worth 2, 1 or 0 marks.

How to decide

Remember that a good answer will:

- do more than simply identify a feature of sentence structure
- go beyond explaining the general function of a feature such as a colon, parenthesis, etc.
- comment on how the feature is used *in this specific example*
- deal with the most important part of the question: how the feature of sentence structure *reinforces the writer's opinion.*

Answer	Mark awarded	Strengths/weaknesses
1. The sentence structure is effective as the writer uses parenthesis and a minor sentence.		
2. This is effective as the writer uses parenthesis to include an extra comment to show how bad Darien was.		
3. The writer's use of sentence structure is effective as the minor sentence ('Except Scotland.') is used to create a strong contrast with the previous statement (that the rest of the world has forgotten Darien). This conveys the writer's opinion that the Scots had made a serious error in going there.		
4. The writer uses parenthesis to insert his own comment in the midst of the fourth sentence ('quite rightly'). This shows that he is endorsing the opinion that the rest of the world was correct to show little interest in this remote place.		

For practice

For each of these extracts, answer the question that follows.

Question

Explain how the writers of these extracts use sentence structure effectively.

Hints

- **Don't** simply identify a feature that is used, without making any further comment on *how* it is used.
- **Don't** make vague comments like 'this is effective' or 'the writer uses repetition for emphasis'.
- **Do** identify a feature of sentence structure and then go on to explain what you think the writer achieves by using this technique.
- **Do** develop your answers by saying 'this is effective *because…*' or 'the writer uses this technique *to emphasise that…*'

1. Let every nation know, whether it wishes us well or ill, that we shall pay any price, bear any burden, meet any hardship, support any friend, oppose any foe to assure the survival and success of liberty.

(*Source:* John F. Kennedy, 20 January 1961)

2. The second and the third day passed, and still my tormentor came not. Once again I breathed as a free man. The monster, in terror, had fled the premises for ever! I should behold it no more! My happiness was supreme!

(*Source: Frankenstein* by Mary Shelley)

→

→

3. Had you rather Caesar were living and die all slaves, than that Caesar were dead, to live all free men? As Caesar loved me, I weep for him; as he was fortunate, I rejoice at it; as he was valiant, I honour him; but, as he was ambitious, I slew him.

(*Source: Julius Caesar* by William Shakespeare)

4. If my books had been any worse, I should not have been invited to Hollywood, and if they had been any better, I should not have come.

(*Source:* Raymond Chandler)

5. I often played in the back courts at Shettleston with Johnny and Joe, one of several pairs of inseparables in my class at Eastbank. We played at tig and jumped from the wash-houses, but it was something different that kept them playing there when we might have been somewhere else. They refused to tell me what it was, but they kept hinting about it, and often with the undertone of dispute. I asked them what the secret was, but the one thing they agreed on was that nobody else could ever know about it. Then Johnny told me when Joe wasn't there. It was a girl.

(*Source: Dancing in the Streets* by Clifford Hanley)

6. Fog everywhere. Fog up the river, where it flows among green airs and meadows; fog down the river, where it rolls defiled among the tiers of shipping, and the waterside pollutions of a great (and dirty) city. Fog on the Essex marshes, fog on the Kentish heights. Fog creeping into the cabooses of collier-brigs; fog lying out on the yards, and hovering in the rigging of great ships; fog drooping on the gunwales of barges and small boats.

(*Source: Bleak House* by Charles Dickens)

7. With mother I was beyond reason. I continually criticised her, corrected her and quarrelled with her every day. I even threw her own china at her.

(*Source:* Mary Kenny)

8. With this faith we will be able to work together, to pray together, to struggle together, to go to jail together, to climb up for freedom together, knowing that we will be free one day.

(*Source:* Martin Luther King, 28 August 1963)

9. Walter Scott was generous. But he was prudent too. Anxious to secure comfort for his family – he now had four children – he invested his savings in Ballantyne's printing business. Thus he became a partner in a venture which might have been successful but for two factors: Ballantyne's inability to size up a business situation, and Scott's inability to size up Ballantyne.

10. In they all came, one after another: some shyly, some boldly, some gracefully, some awkwardly, some pushing, some pulling; in they all came, anyhow and everyhow. Away they all went, twenty couples at once: hands half round and back again the other way; down the middle and up again; round and round in various stages of affectionate grouping; old top couple always turning up in the wrong place; new top couple starting off again, as soon as they got there; all top couples at last and not a bottom one to help them.

(*Source: A Christmas Carol* by Charles Dickens)

(There are more examples for practice in analysing sentence structure questions at the end of Appendix I: Grammar and syntax.)

Checklist for tackling structure questions

Sentence type:

- Can you identify the five types of sentence: statement, question, exclamation, command and minor sentence?

Sentence length:

- Does the author vary the lengths of his or her sentences?
- What does he or she achieve by doing this?

Punctuation:

- How is punctuation used to divide up the sentence?
- Are question marks, exclamation marks, inverted commas, dashes, colons or semi-colons used for particular effects?
- Does the author make use of parenthesis?

Pattern:

- Do you notice anything about the order of the words, such as inversion or repetition?
- Is there an element of balance or balanced contrast (antithesis) between different parts of the sentence?
- Does the author use lists?
- Does a list lead to a climax or an anti-climax?

WORD CHOICE

Analyse how the writer's word choice conveys...

Before you answer questions on a writer's word choice in a piece of writing, it is helpful to establish two things:

- Is it written in a **formal** or an **informal** style?
- Is the word choice **literal** or **figurative**?

By the end of this section you should have a clear understanding of these terms.

Formal and informal language

It is possible to convey the same piece of information in very different styles of language.

For example, the list of by-laws for a tennis club might state that:

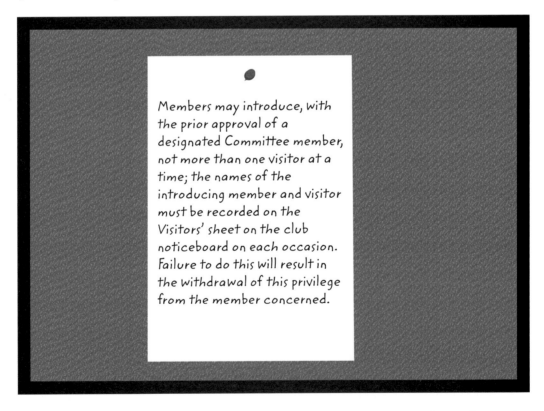

Members may introduce, with the prior approval of a designated Committee member, not more than one visitor at a time; the names of the introducing member and visitor must be recorded on the Visitors' sheet on the club noticeboard on each occasion. Failure to do this will result in the withdrawal of this privilege from the member concerned.

On the other hand, if the Club President sees a player disregarding the rule, he or she might say:

If you don't write your names on the noticeboard, you'll not be allowed to bring your friend again.

The basic meaning is the same in both cases but the language of the first example is very formal while the second is informal.

What are the differences between the two examples? Use the following table as a checklist.

Formal	Informal
Longer, more complex sentence structures; grammatically correct, complete sentences.	Simpler, looser sentence structures; minor sentences (note form).
No abbreviations.	Use of shortened forms, e.g. 'don't'; 'you'll'.
Wide range of word choice, including complex or technical vocabulary; words with Latin/Greek roots.	Common, everyday words, some perhaps non-standard English, such as slang or dialect forms.
Use of 'literary' punctuation marks, such as colons and semi-colons.	Simple punctuation marks, such as commas. Exclamation marks are more typical of informal writing.
Impersonal tone. The author does not address the reader directly as 'you' or attempt to relate to the reader's feelings.	Personal approach (using first person 'I' and second person 'you'), i.e. subjective.
Does not attempt to be humorous.	Chatty, conversational tone. Expresses feelings. May be humorous.
Tends to be factual. Likely to be objective (taking a balanced and unbiased stance.)	Tends to express thoughts, feelings and opinions.

Within the general division into formal/informal language, there are a number of other related terms that you should know.

Register, jargon and rhetoric

Register

This is a term meaning a type of language used in a particular setting or by a particular group of people. For example, you might be asked how the 'register' in one section of a text contrasts with another. A possible answer might be that one is formal and the other informal. Another possibility is that one might be expressed in the complex, technical language used by a professional group, while the other might be in relatively simple, everyday language accessible to the general reader.

Jargon

This is a specialised type of formal language including technical terms relating to a particular subject or occupation. For instance, terms such as *byte*, *icon*, *dialogue box*, *file menu*, *monitor* and *font* belong to the jargon of computing. Clearly, an expert needs to use such vocabulary in the course of his or her work or studies.

The term 'jargon', however, can also have negative associations, and is sometimes used to describe the use of unnecessarily complex and obscure words in an attempt to sound impressive. This amusing example of a conversation between a probation officer and a judge was quoted in the correspondence column of a newspaper:

Probation officer: He hails from a multi-delinquent family with a high incarceration index.

Judge: You mean the whole lot are inside?

Probation officer: Inter-sibling rivalry hindered his ongoing relationships making him an isolate in a stress situation with his peers.

Judge: You mean that he hated his brothers?

Rhetoric

Rhetorical language is another aspect of formal English. Such language aims to give an elevated, dignified and impressive effect and is typically used in delivering a formal speech, as for example by a politician addressing a conference (in fact, the word 'rhetoric' means the art of public speaking). Repetition and emotive language (see pages 51–53) are typical devices used. A favourite technique used by such speakers is to phrase a statement in the form of a question (**rhetorical question**). The speaker is not really asking the audience to answer and the listeners already know what the speaker's answer would be:

Shall we relax our efforts at the very moment when victory is in our grasp?

Here, the expected answer is obviously, 'No'.

Dialect

Dialect depends on geography, and refers to a way of speaking that is limited to a particular town or district.

For practice

If you have read *Sunset Song,* you will be familiar with Lewis Grassic Gibbon's use of the particular dialect of the Scots language spoken in the early twentieth century in the Mearns, a rural district in north-east Scotland.

Lewis Grassic Gibbon (1901–35, real name, Leslie Mitchell)

> Now, Peesie's Knapp's biggings were not more than twenty years old, but gey ill-favoured for all that,… the house faced the road – and that was fair handy if it didn't scunner you that you couldn't so much as change your sark without some ill-fashioned brute gowking in at you.
>
> (*Source: Sunset Song* by Lewis Grassic Gibbon)

Question

Can you translate this into modern standard English?

The contemporary Scottish writer William McIlvanney, in novels such as *Docherty*, has put Lanarkshire dialect into a written form to give an authentic feel to the dialogue:

Ah'm sorry Ah hiv tae turn ye doon. Ye're guid but ye're auld, son.

(*Source: Docherty* by William McIlvanney)

Writers sometimes use dialect in non-fiction writing to add local colour or a touch of humour.

Michael Munro has made an in-depth study of Glasgow 'patter' and has collected enough examples of it to fill two books, *The Patter* and *The Patter, Another Blast*. He believes that dialect develops because it is 'a common form of identity'. He has suggested:

For the homesick it is a concrete link with home. It is the medium for shared humour, remembered songs and poems, catchphrases, and greetings that will always identify you more truly than any passport photograph.

(*Source: The Patter, Another Blast* by Michael Munro)

Glasgow skyline

Slang

Slang is the name given to extremely colloquial words and expressions that are not generally considered acceptable for use in formal speech situations, such as TV news bulletins or job interviews. Examples would be 'whacked' (instead of 'tired') or 'kids' (for 'children'). The degree of acceptability of such language is on a sliding scale, from terms that would seem mildly inappropriate in formal situations to vulgar expressions that would be completely unacceptable.

Some slang is typical of a particular period or age group. For example, in the 1920s, 'ripping' was a slang term of approval. In the sixties, 'groovy' and 'fab' were used in the same way. More recently, 'wicked' and 'bad' were used in street slang to mean the opposite of their dictionary definitions.

Slang varies from one English-speaking country to another, and new forms are constantly evolving. Can you think of examples of current American and Australian slang you may have heard in TV or films?

Writers sometimes use slang to provide a humorous contrast with more formal expression.

For practice

In the following extract from James Herriot's *Vet in a Spin*, a woman finally decides to bring her dog to the vet for treatment after her husband has tried all kinds of home-made remedies. Read the extract and then answer the questions that follow it.

'Just look at me good dog, Mr Herriot!' she rapped out. I looked.

'Good heavens!' I gasped.

The little animal was almost completely bald. His skin was dry, scaly and wrinkled, and his head hung down as though he were under sedation.

'Aye, you're surprised, aren't you?' she barked. 'He's in a terrible state, isn't he?'

'I'm afraid so. I wouldn't have known him.'

'No, nobody would. Ah think the world o' this dog and just look at 'im!' She paused and snorted a few times. 'And I know who's responsible, don't you?'

'Well…'

'Oh, you do. It's that husband o' mine.' She paused and glared at me, breathing rapidly. 'What d'you think of my husband, Mr Herriot?'

'I really don't know him very well. I…'

'Well, ah know 'im and he's a gawp. He's a great gawp. Knows everything and knows nowt. He's played around wi' me good dog till he's ruined 'im.'

I didn't say anything. I was studying the keeshound. It was the first time I had been able to observe him closely and I was certain I knew the cause of his trouble.

Mrs Pilling stuck her jaw out further and continued. 'First me husband said it was eczema. Is it?'

'No.'

'Then 'e said it was mange. Is it?'

'No.'

'D'you know what it is?'

'Yes.'

'Well, will you tell me please?'

'It's myxoedema.'

'Myx…?'

'Wait a minute,' I said. 'I'll just make absolutely sure.' I reached for my stethoscope and put it on the dog's chest. And the bradycardia was there as I expected, the slow, slow heartbeat of hypothyroidism. 'Yes, that's it. Not a shadow of a doubt about it.'

'What did you call it?'

'Myxoedema. It's a thyroid deficiency – there's a gland in his neck which isn't doing its job properly.'

'And that makes 'is hair fall out?'

'Oh yes. And it also causes this typical scaliness and wrinkling of the skin.'

'Aye, but he's half asleep all t'time. How about that?'

'Another classic symptom. Dogs with this condition become very lethargic – lose all their energy.'

She reached out and touched the dog's skin, bare and leathery where once the coat had grown in bushy glory. 'And can you cure it?'

'Yes.'

'Now Mr Herriot, don't take this the wrong way, but could you be mistaken? Are ye positive it's this myxi-whatever-it-is?'

'Of course I am. It's a straightforward case.'

→

'Straightforward to you, maybe.' She flushed and appeared to be grinding her teeth. 'But not straightforward to that clever husband o' mine. The great lubbert! When ah think what he's put me good dog through – ah could kill 'im.'

(*Source: Vet in a Spin* by James Herriot)

Questions

Pick out two or three examples each from the extract of:
a) informal language or slang
b) dialect
c) jargon.
Draw a table and enter your examples in the appropriate columns. Examples are given to start you off.

Informal language or slang	Dialect	Jargon
Good heavens!	He's a gawp	Myxoedema

Task

For discussion

Divide a sheet of paper into three columns, headed Dialect, Slang or informal English, and Formal English.

Working in pairs, write down in the first column a list of expressions you are familiar with that are used in your local area.

Next, 'translate' these into conversational English and then, if possible, into a formal style with the same meaning.

Which of the three is most effective in each case? Does stating a point in a certain way make it more humorous, forceful or impressive?

Literal and figurative language

Although the tennis club rules, the probation report and the story about the vet vary widely in their degree of formality, all are examples of language being used to convey information in a *literal* way. This means that words are being used to mean exactly what they say: their use corresponds to the definitions you would find if you looked them up in a dictionary.

Remember

A simple way of working out whether a word is being used literally or figuratively is to ask whether the thing is actually physically present, or whether it is brought in by way of comparison.

Obviously, most language is used in this sense, but words can also be used in a non-literal way. In everyday conversation we use expressions like these:

She's only trying to wind you up – don't rise to the bait!

Keep practising – maybe you'll be a big star one day!

Here the physical objects ('bait', 'star') are not actually the real subject of discussion but are brought in by way of comparison. These words are being used *figuratively* or *metaphorically*.

For practice

Let every nation know, whether it wishes us well or ill, that we shall pay any price, bear any burden, meet any hardship, support any friend, oppose any foe to assure the survival and success of liberty.

(*Source:* John F. Kennedy, 20 January 1961)

Question

Look again at the quotation from President John F. Kennedy above.

With a partner, discuss Kennedy's word choice and work out where words are being used literally and where they are being used figuratively.

IMAGERY

There are many different kinds of figurative language – often called *figures of speech* or *imagery* – and you will already have met some of these, perhaps in the course of studying poetry. Three in particular – **simile**, **metaphor** and **personification** – attempt to paint a clearer picture of what something is like by comparing it to another, basically dissimilar, object (known as the '**image**') with which it has one or more similarities.

Simile

A **simile** is a comparison in which one thing is said to be **like** something else ('A' *is like* 'B'). The word 'as' can also be used in comparing the two things.

Laurie Lee uses the following simile to describe how passers-by reacted when he played his violin in the street for the first time:

It was as though the note of the fiddle touched some subconscious nerve that had to be answered – like a baby's cry.

(*Source: As I Walked Out One Midsummer Morning* by Laurie Lee)

The 'note of the fiddle' is the real subject; the 'baby's cry' is not actually heard but is the image brought in as a comparison. A crying baby cannot be ignored; in the same way, the pedestrians felt compelled to react to the music. Like the note of the violin, a baby's cry is high pitched and penetrating. There is also a basic *dissimilarity* between the two things compared, however: the sound of a violin comes from an inanimate musical instrument, while the baby's cry is a human voice.

Remember

Not every comparison using the words 'like' or 'as' is a figurative use of language: 'The scenery of Ireland is like the Highlands of Scotland' is not a simile as it is simply a comparison between two similar, literal subjects. There is no real *dissimilarity* between them. In addition, if the thing being compared *could actually be* the subject, it is not a simile: 'A large bird like a crow flapped down.' Since the bird might actually be a crow this is not a true simile, just a descriptive phrase. 'The cloaked priest flapped in like a crow', however, would be a simile, as there are points of dissimilarity (human/bird; large/small) as well as similarity (e.g. black colour, sense of menace.)

Metaphor

In the case of metaphor, something is spoken of as if it is another thing (known as 'the image') with which it has one or more points of similarity; the effect is striking precisely because of the points of *dissimilarity*. In a metaphor, the word 'like' or 'as' is not used. The subject is said **to be** the figurative comparison ('A' *is* 'B'). On his travels in Spain, Laurie Lee met an attractive girl who was a fanatical communist. He uses the following metaphor to describe her:

Her lovely mouth was a political megaphone.

(*Source: As I Walked Out One Midsummer Morning* by Laurie Lee)

The girl's mouth – or voice – is the **literal** subject and the 'political megaphone' is the **image**, brought in as a **figurative** comparison to emphasise not just that she talks non-stop about politics, but that she does so in a loud and perhaps aggressive manner. The 'megaphone' **image** is used by the writer to convey this idea in a concise and striking way.

Extended metaphor

Writers sometimes sustain and develop one comparison over several lines. Here, Jonathan Miller, TV broadcaster and medical doctor, is discussing the circulation of the blood:

Unlike the wealth of a miser, which accumulates without its doing any useful work, the value of blood is beyond price as long as it visits and revisits every part of the body. How does this treasure work? In what currency are its transactions conducted? What are its denominations?

(*Source: The Body in Question* by Jonathan Miller)

This technique is known as an **extended metaphor**. The initial image of wealth is continued in the sentences that follow by using other words connected with money, such as 'beyond price', 'treasure', 'currency', 'transactions' and 'denominations'.

Mixed metaphor

This term is used when two or more images are confused, to ridiculous effect. Recently, the manager of a Scottish football club said during an interview:

'We played well in the first half, but in the second half our Achilles heel came back to bite us.'

Personification

Personification is a special type of metaphor in which an inanimate object is given human characteristics, moods, reactions and so on. This figure of speech is often used in descriptions of nature, as in Tennyson's poem 'The Lady of Shalott':

The broad stream in his banks complaining.

(*Source:* 'The Lady of Shalott' by Alfred Lord Tennyson)

A river cannot *actually* 'complain': the personification is used to indicate that the water seemed noisy, restless and turbulent *as if* it felt dissatisfied.

As these examples would suggest, figurative language is used in literature to help readers appreciate more clearly particular aspects of the subject being described.

What the examiner is looking for

Analyse how the writer's use of imagery helps you understand…

In tackling similar questions, ask yourself:

- What is the image, i.e. what is the subject being compared to?
- What is the nature of the image – in what way is it similar to the subject?
- How does the comparison help you to appreciate the subject more fully?

Look at the following example of a metaphor, which comes from Shakespeare's *Othello*. The speaker is the villain, Iago, who plans to bring down his rival, Cassio, by hinting that he is having an affair with Othello's wife, Desdemona.

With as little a web as this I will ensnare as great a fly as Cassio.

(*Source: Othello* by William Shakespeare)

Here are the steps by which you could arrive at a good answer for the question in the box above:

* The image is of a spider catching a fly in a web.

* In the same way, Iago intends to entrap Cassio through his lies and insinuations.

* The metaphor helps you appreciate the malicious, predatory nature of Iago and his scheme. Many people find spiders loathsome, and Iago will appear equally disgusting.

Answer

Having clarified these three points in your mind, you can now devise an answer, such as:

Just as a spider spins a web in order to catch flies for prey, so Iago intends to entrap Cassio by his lies and insinuations. This arouses disgust in the audience both for the malice it reveals and because many people find spiders horrible.

> ### Hint
>
> Here is a way of laying out an answer on imagery:
>
> * Just as … so…
> * This helps the reader appreciate/ understand…

For practice

> ### Question
>
> Bearing in mind the advice given on the previous pages, comment on the effectiveness of the writers' use of imagery in the following examples.

> ### Note
>
> In this exercise, you should focus solely on imagery. You may, however, wish to widen your discussion to include other language features when you go over your completed answers.

1. A house like this became a dinosaur, occupying too much ground and demanding to be fed new sinks and drainpipes and a sea of electricity. Such a house became a fossil, stranded among neighbours long since chopped up into flats and bed-sitting rooms.

(*Source: The House in Norham Gardens by Penelope Lively*)

2. The gas-mantle putted like a sick man's heart. Dimmed to a bead of light, it made the room mysterious as a chapel. The polished furniture, enriched by darkness, entombed fragments of the firelight that moved like tapers in a tunnel. The brasses glowed like icons.

(*Source: Docherty by William McIlvanney*)

3. My instructor, one of Seville's most respected professors of the guitar, was a small, sad man, exquisitely polite and patient. Each day, at the stroke of ten, he knocked softly at my door and entered on tiptoe, as though into a sick room, carrying his guitar-case like a doctor's bag.

   'How are we today?' he would ask sympathetically, 'and how do we proceed?' After an hour's examination, during which he tested all my faulty co-ordinations, he would hand me a page of exercises and bid me take them twice a day.

(*Source: A Rose for Winter by Laurie Lee*)

➜

4. (*In this story R.L. Stevenson is describing an attack on an antiques shop dealer by a man called Markheim.*)

    'This, perhaps, may suit,' observed the dealer and then, as he began to re-arise, Markheim bounded from behind upon his victim. The long, skewer-like dagger flashed and fell. The dealer struggled like a hen, striking his temple on the shelf, and then tumbled to the floor in a heap… In those poor miserly clothes, in that ungainly attitude, the dealer lay like so much sawdust.

(*Source:* 'Markheim' by R.L. Stevenson)

5. The rain raced along horizontally, sticking into them like glass splinters till they were wet through.

(*Source: Tess of the d'Urbervilles* by Thomas Hardy)

6. (*This extract provides a description of women MPs heckling the Prime Minster.*)

    This was like the opening day of the Debenhams sales combined with a St Trinian's lacrosse match.

(*Source:* Quentin Letts, *Daily Mail*)

7. At Prime Minister's Questions, the Opposition scratched for misery like hens pecking at dirt.

(*Source:* Quentin Letts, *Daily Mail*)

8. Houses above looked caught on the scraggly hillsides like crumbs in a beard and apt to fall as suddenly.

(*Source: Winter's Bone* by Daniel Woodrell)

9. The Defence Secretary is what is known as 'a safe pair of hands'. In other words, he is intensely boring. At the dispatch box, anyway. In private, he may be the liveliest company you could wish for, his conversation as light and heady as the first flute of champagne.

(*Source:* Michael Deacon, *Daily Telegraph*)

10. I became more and more alienated, bored with the inane chatter. *The Apprentice* runner-up was as hyperactive as a bee in a jam jar.

(*Source:* Liz Jones, *Daily Mail*)

11. It is one of the oldest tricks in any dog's repertoire, enthusiastically chasing a stick or a ball and retrieving it for its owner. But the time-honoured game of 'fetch' could soon be hounded out of parks in Glasgow under proposals by council bosses for dogs to be kept on leads or 'close at heel'. An owner said, 'Dogs need to be able to belt about to let off steam. This Stalinist proposal would appear to condemn an entire urban canine population to ennui because of a few rotten apples.'

(*Source:* Aimee Beveridge, *Daily Mail*)

12. The new incumbent, struggling for words which would do justice to the immensity of the task facing him as he took over the managership of Newcastle United, said: 'It is time to plug the leak-holes, batten down the hatches and get the ship sailing again.' It was enough to make the non-sailors among us reach for the Kwells and I felt a bit queasy myself as I listened. What are they running at St James' Park – some sort of ark?

(*Source:* Ian Wood, *The Scotsman*)

Other figures of speech and literary terms

There are many other literary techniques that can loosely be classified as **figures of speech**. This term can include almost any use of language to achieve some kind of special effect beyond the basic function of conveying information. Some of these figures of speech relate more to the sound of the word than to its meaning, which is why such techniques are often to be found in poetry; other figures of speech have to do with exaggeration. It would probably be safe to say that what they all have in common is that the writer's main concern is less with the straightforward literal meaning of the words than with the achievement of a particular effect. The effect might be descriptive, or humorous, or sarcastic, or emphatic, and so on.

The following list of definitions will be useful for reference and will help you to answer questions like:

> Explain the effectiveness of…

Although it is not necessary to know *all* of these terms, you will find that it is often simpler to identify a technique by its proper name rather than struggling to explain it in another way. For convenience, these terms have been grouped into four categories:

- Sound effects
- Overstating, understating and talking in circles
- Contrasts, opposites and contradictions
- The new, the old and the overused.

Sound effects

Alliteration

This is usually defined as a series of words in which the same letter is repeated, usually at the beginning of two or more words. Remember, however, that as with all literary techniques, the writer must be doing it deliberately to create a particular effect.

Once you have been introduced to the idea of alliteration, you may start to find examples of it everywhere! As there are only 26 letters in the alphabet, it is inevitable that in some sentences there will be several words with the same initial letter.

For example, 'He carried the box of books up to the storeroom on the top floor of the building.' There are three words beginning with 'b' here, but all of them are simple nouns and there does not appear to be any particular literary effect intended.

When the travel writer Patrick Leigh-Fermor, in describing a town in Holland, talks about the 'clip-clop of clogs on the cobblestones', however, the alliteration is clearly deliberate: you can almost hear the rhythmical sound of the wooden shoes on the street.

Onomatopoeia

This is the name given to words that imitate the sound they are describing. You may have noticed that this figure of speech often works in conjunction with alliteration. For example, in the above quotation, the alliteration helps to create an onomatopoeic effect.

This is how D.H. Lawrence describes a snake drinking from a water trough in his poem 'Snake':

He sipped with his straight mouth,

Softly drank through his straight gums, into his slack long body,

Silently.

(*Source:* 'Snake' by D.H. Lawrence)

The alliteration of the letter 's' (also known as **sibilance**) creates a 'hissing' effect appropriate to a description of a snake. The effect of a series of pleasing sounds is known as **euphony**. A neatly turned phrase like 'incorrigible but thoroughly irresistible' on page 86 is said to be **euphonious**.

Pun

Sometimes called a 'play on words', a pun is created by using words that sound similar but have different meanings. The effect intended is usually a humorous one, although there are plenty of bad jokes that depend on puns!

'Waiter!'

'Yes sir?'

'What's this supposed to be?'

'It's bean soup, sir.'

'I don't care what it's been. What is it now?'

Overstating, understating and talking in circles

Hyperbole

Hyperbole is deliberate exaggeration in order to emphasise the point being made – often for a humorous effect. The Australian writer Clive James often used this technique with great skill. Describing the film actor Marlon Brando as 'Hollywood's number one broody outcast', he said that:

He could order a cheeseburger with fries and make it sound like a challenge to the Establishment.

(*Source: Fame in the 20th Century* by Clive James)

Marlon Brando

Litotes

Litotes or **understatement** is the opposite of hyperbole. In *My Family and Other Animals*, the naturalist Gerald Durrell wrote of his mother:

On Monday morning I found her in the garage being pursued round and round by an irate pelican which she was trying to feed with sardines from a tin.

'I'm glad you've come, dear,' she panted; 'this pelican is a little difficult to handle.'

(*Source: My Family and Other Animals* by Gerald Durrell)

As with so many other figures of speech, hyperbole and litotes are not confined to writing but are often used in everyday conversation:

Isn't there anything to drink? I'm dying of thirst! (Hyperbole)

The teacher wasn't exactly overjoyed when I told her that I'd left my work at home. (Litotes)

Euphemism

This is a way of making an unwelcome truth seem less harsh or unpleasant by dressing it up in inoffensive language. Many euphemisms are connected with the subject of death, as when we say that someone has 'passed away' rather than 'died'. In 1948, the novelist Evelyn Waugh wrote a novel called *The Loved One* that makes fun of American funeral customs, in the course of which he uses many euphemisms, such as 'leave-taking', 'Slumber Room', 'Whispering Glades' and 'Before Need Provision Arrangements'. Can you guess what some of these terms might refer to?

Euphemisms are equally plentiful in the world of politics. One of the most famous examples came from the 1950s' Prime Minister, Sir Anthony Eden, who once said: 'We are not at war with Egypt. We are in a state of armed conflict.'

Circumlocution

This literally means 'to talk round' something – in other words, to state something in a long, roundabout way rather than addressing the subject simply and directly. The nineteenth-century novelist Charles Dickens poked fun at lawyers and government officials for doing this (see page 51).

Contrasts, opposites and contradictions

Paradox

A statement that appears to be a contradiction but which, on closer examination, does contain a truth. For example, 'To preserve the peace, prepare for war' seems to be a contradiction, but it is based on the 'deterrent' idea that if one side builds up its military strength then the enemy will not dare to attack, and thus peace will be maintained. This oft-quoted comment by Oscar Wilde is another example of paradox:

Nowadays people know the price of everything, and the value of nothing.

(*Source: The Picture of Dorian Gray* by Oscar Wilde)

Oxymoron

A condensed form of paradox, in which two opposites are placed side by side to heighten the effect of contrast. Edwin Muir's poem 'The Horses' ends with horses coming to a group of human survivors of a nuclear war and voluntarily allowing themselves to be used to plough the land: the poet describes their action as 'free servitude'. (If this poem is in your poetry book, read it and try to work out the significance of this oxymoron.)

Juxtaposition

This simply means placing side by side. In the above example of oxymoron, it could be said that the two opposites are placed **in juxtaposition**. A writer might deliberately place two sentences beside each other to highlight the contrast between them. Here is another example from Clive James' book on fame; in this case, the juxtaposition creates an antithesis (see page 26) with a very entertaining effect:

Dustin Hoffman became famous in the sixties in *The Graduate* playing a nervous young man who sus-pected that life in America was stacked against him. In the seventies he became more famous still as an even more nervous, slightly less young man, who knew that life in America was stacked against him.

(*Source: Fame in the 20th Century* by Clive James)

The new, the old and the overused

Neologism

The coining of a new word, usually to describe a recent development or invention for which an appropriate term does not exist. Many recent examples come from the internet, e.g. 'cyberspace' and 'flashmob' (a group summoned quickly), or from the technical development of mobile phones, such as 'selfie' (a photograph of oneself taken with the mobile phone camera). The language of texting or 'textspeak' is constantly evolving, examples being mainly forms of abbreviation, e.g. 'njoy' (enjoy) and 'f2f' (face to face), or **acronyms**, words formed from the initial letters of a phrase, such as 'AFAIK' (as far as I know).

Archaism

Whereas a neologism is a newly invented word, an archaism denotes a word or phrase from the past that is no longer in current use but is still generally understood. For example:

Arm thyself lightly, mount to horse, keep thy land, aid thy men, hurtle into the press. Thou needest not to strike another, neither to be smitten down.

(*Source: Aucassin & Nicolette and Other Mediaeval Romances and Legends* by Eugene Mason)

A writer may adopt an archaic style in order to recapture the feel of a historical period, or to affect the tone in some way – e.g. to create irony or humour. Archaic spelling can also be used in this way: 'ye olde inne'.

Cliché

An expression that at one time might have been original but has now become overused, such as 'in this day and age' or 'all part and parcel of'. Well-worn similes like 'as white as snow' are clichés and should be avoided *like the plague* (another cliché!).

For practice

Questions

Working individually or in pairs:

- Identify which of the above literary techniques are used in the following extracts. Remember that more than one technique might be used in each case.

- Consider why the writer has used that technique. What effect is he or she trying to achieve?

1. Recently I found myself unimpressed by some visiting Americans who came and saw and stunned with monstrous verbosity, determined to use five words where one would do, bent on calling a canteen an 'in-plant feeding situation' and a spade 'a primitive earth-breaking implement.'

   (*Source: Daily Mail*)

2. It was a morning of mysterious monotones: black rocks above and a black sea beneath.

   (*Source: A Rose for Winter, by Laurie Lee*)

3. Christmas found me

   with other fond and foolish girls

   at the menswear counters

   shopping for the ties that bind.

   (*Source: 'Obituary' by Liz Lochhead*)

4. Easter eggs and hot cross buns from supermarkets have beaten the best that luxury food firms have to offer. A £25 Tesco egg is top of the chocs.

   (*Source: Daily Mail*)

5. (*A description of Johnny Weismuller, the actor who became famous in the role of Tarzan.*)

   He started off as an Olympic swimmer who won so many medals he could stay fit just carrying them around.

   (*Source: Fame in the 20th Century by Clive James*)

➡

6. *Member of Parliament:* Is the government still intent on implementing these savage cuts, which will strike at the very fabric of our society?

    Government minister: We are carrying out an in-depth examination of current expenditure to see if economies can be made that will ultimately benefit the taxpayer.

7. 'I have our brochure here setting out our services. Were you thinking of interment or incineration?'

    'Pardon me?'

    'Buried or burned?'

(*Source: The Loved One* by Evelyn Waugh)

8. 'I would speak with you, Sir Minstrel,' said the young knight. 'If thou dost not find the air of this morning too harsh, heartily do I wish thou wouldst fairly tell me what can have induced thee, being, as thou seemest, a man of sense, to thrust thyself into a wild country like this, at such a time.'

(*Source: The Waverley Novels* by Sir Walter Scott)

9. It was a game of two halves. United set out their stall early doors to soak up City's pressure and hit on the break; however, they flirted with disaster and only a crunching tackle by sweeper Jonson on striker Smith as the latter was about to pull the trigger kept the scores level. Towards the interval, City did score twice through Klein, leaving United a mountain to climb.

    In the second half it all went pear-shaped for City. United kept their heads down and White scored two fine goals to throw his team a lifeline. The United manager was over the moon, declaring his team had literally given one hundred and ten per cent. His counterpart at City was as sick as a parrot.

(*Source:* N. McDermott)

10. Given the nature of the hotel I'd expected the menu to feature items like brown Windsor soup and roast beef and Yorkshire pudding, but of course things have moved on in the hotel trade. The menu now was richly endowed with words that you wouldn't have seen on a menu ten years ago – 'noisettes', 'tartare', 'duxelle', 'coulis', 'timbale' – and written in a curious inflated language with eccentric capitalizations. I had, and I quote, 'Fanned Galia Melon and Cumbrian Air-dried Ham served with a Mixed Leaf Salad' followed by 'Fillet Steak served with a Crushed Black Peppercorn Sauce flamed in Brandy and finished with Cream', which together were nearly as pleasurable to read as to eat.

    I was greatly taken with this new way of talking and derived considerable pleasure from speaking it to the waiter. I asked him for a lustre of water freshly drawn from the house tap and presented au nature in a cylinder of glass, and when he came round with the bread rolls I entreated him to present me with a tongued rondel of blanched wheat oven-baked and masked in a poppy-seed coating. I was just getting warmed up to this and about to ask for a fanned lap coverlet, freshly laundered and scented with a delicate hint of Persil, to replace the one that had slipped from my lap and now lay recumbent on the horizontal walking surface anterior to my feet when he handed me a card that said 'Sweets Menu' and I realized that we were back in the no-nonsense world of English.

(*Source: Notes from a Small Island* by Bill Bryson)

TONE

Many Higher English candidates find questions on tone difficult to answer – mainly because they don't understand what is being asked for.

> **Comment on the tone of...** (1 mark)

Tone does not relate directly to meaning but rather to the *way* in which something is said. It refers to a particular attitude or feeling being conveyed by the writer.

Consider a simple question:

Where have you been?

These words could be spoken in various situations:

- By someone talking to a friend who has recently been on holiday.
- By someone talking to a friend who has not been seen for a long time.
- By a parent to a teenage son or daughter who arrives home at 4 a.m.

Exactly the same words might be used but they would be said in quite different ways. This is what is meant by tone.

For practice

Task

1. In pairs, try reading the question below aloud as you feel it might be said in order to convey a particular attitude or emotion.
   Where have you been?
   Your partner should try to guess what tone you are adopting. You might try to express anger, surprise, sarcasm, resentment, mockery, impatience, bewilderment, etc.

2. Try the same exercise with one or two other simple sentences you have made up yourselves.

3. 'I'm so glad you didn't wait, Agnes,' Mr Logan said, in a tone that clearly said, 'I think you might have waited.'
   Can you deliver Mr Logan's words in this tone?

The journalist and humourist Craig Brown was focusing on tone when he wrote about the word 'sorry' to mark its hundredth anniversary in the English dictionary as a 'stand-alone' word of apology.

'"Sorry" seems to be the hardest word' sang Elton John, but the opposite is closer to the truth: sorry seems to be the easiest word – except, perhaps, when we really mean it.

Of course, 'sorry' is a word with a great multitude of meanings. The British should really have as many words for 'sorry' as Eskimos have words for snow, particularly as we so rarely use it as a sincere expression of regret.

→

> A quizzical 'Sorry?' means 'I didn't hear you.'
>
> Said slightly louder – 'Sorry?!' – means 'I must have misheard you because otherwise what you have just said is incomprehensible to me.'
>
> An exasperated 'Sor-reee!' means 'You are over-reacting and I'm not really to blame.'
>
> In a restaurant, 'Sorry' as in 'Sorry, we've been waiting half an hour and our starter still hasn't arrived', really means 'I'm furious.'
>
> In an argument, the 'sorry' in 'Sorry, that is not what I'm saying', means 'You liar.'
>
> And on a current affairs programme, 'Sorry, I'm going to have to hurry you' means 'Get on with it, you old windbag.'
>
> (*Source:* Craig Brown, *Daily Mail*)

In speech, the tone of voice used makes the speaker's feelings clear. In writing, however, you must look at the word choice to find clues to the feelings or attitude of the author.

Serious or humorous?

It would be impossible to list every nuance of tone that a writer might use, as there are as many as there are attitudes. But they can be broadly categorised into three types.

Light-hearted

A **light-hearted** tone will often include informal and conversational language.

The word **conversational** itself can describe a tone, particularly a **chatty, friendly** tone, as if the writer is confiding in a friend. The pronoun 'you' is likely to be used.

An example of a conversational tone is to be found in the opening chapter of *Sunset Song* by Lewis Grassic Gibbon, where the writer is gossiping to the reader about his characters:

Chae … wasn't the quarrelsome kind except when roused, so he was well-liked, though folk laughed at him. But God knows, who is it they don't laugh at?

(*Source: Sunset Song* by Lewis Grassic Gibbon)

The tone may be **humorous** in a straightforward way, where the author is finding his subject funny and he hopes the reader will too.

A **flippant** tone is where the author is showing an irreverent attitude to something normally taken seriously. An example is to be found in Philip Larkin's poem 'Church Going', where the poet enters a church and describes the altar as, 'some brass and stuff, up at the holy end.' Here the use of colloquial and informal expressions conveys his lack of respect.

Ironic

Irony is the name given to the figure of speech where an author says the opposite of what he or she really means. This could be purely for humorous effect, but there is more often a serious purpose behind irony. An author's feelings can be expressed more forcefully for being inverted in this way.

A **sarcastic** or **scathing** tone is one that may use irony in order to criticise or wound its target. It can be an outlet for anger.

A **mocking** tone often uses irony and sarcasm to ridicule something or someone.

A **tongue-in-cheek** tone is also a form of irony: the writer will sound serious, but there will be a sense of ridicule behind this, too. Euphemism is a common feature of this tone. An example might be the expression 'tired and emotional' to mean 'drunk', which the satirical magazine *Private Eye* uses to avoid lawsuits from the prominent people whom it exposes.

A **satirical** tone is an extreme form of irony. Here a writer is funny in a more savage way: he or she holds a subject up to ridicule in order to attack it. This is the tone adopted by George Orwell in *Animal Farm*, for example, where he satirised Russian communists by comparing them to pigs. The satirist's purpose is deeply serious although on the surface he may appear light-hearted.

Serious

A **serious** tone is used for serious purposes, on solemn occasions. Words such as 'earnest', 'formal', 'ponderous' or even 'pompous' might be applied.

A **thoughtful**, **reflective** tone might be used by someone writing about philosophy or religion. It would include abstract nouns and ideas.

A **respectful** tone will tend to use formal expression and vocabulary. It will avoid slang and colloquial English. An example might be a eulogy at a funeral, or a newspaper obituary.

An **emotive** tone will generally be serious. It will play upon the emotions of the reader by using many references to feelings such as anger, shock, sadness and so on.

A **matter-of-fact** tone is the opposite of emotive – it will present information in a deliberately unemotional, impassive way, which can provide an effective contrast to disturbing material, for example when reporting atrocities from a war zone.

A **polemical** tone comes from a Greek word meaning 'war-like' and refers to the kind of rhetorical, rousing language a politician might use to stir up resentment or rebellion.

A **persuasive** tone will be used by writers who want to sell something, whether it be an idea, a point of view or a product.

An **enthusiastic**, effusive tone might be used in an advertisement or a tourist guide book promoting a place. A list of gushing superlatives would be an example of this.

It should be clear that there is a lot of overlap within the three categories. As long as you can identify the correct general category for valid reasons of style and meaning, you should be able to answer tone questions successfully. It is not essential to specify 'tongue-in-cheek' rather than 'mocking' as long as you show awareness of the writer's intention and mood.

Focus on irony

Irony is one of the most common techniques used to convey tone. The most common form of irony is when someone says the opposite of what they really mean. If a friend were to say at the end of the summer holidays, 'I can't wait to get back to school', this would presumably be an example of irony.

A famous example of this kind of irony in literature can be found in Shakespeare's *Julius Caesar*. After Caesar has been assassinated, his right-hand man, Antony, is permitted by Brutus (one of the leaders of the conspiracy against Caesar) to make a speech to the people of Rome. Brutus allows Antony to do this on condition that he does not criticise the conspirators, but Antony cleverly uses irony to make his point, attacking Brutus while apparently praising him:

Here, under leave of Brutus and the rest –

For Brutus is an honourable man;

So are they all, all honourable men –

Come I to speak in Caesar's funeral.

He was my friend, faithful and just to me;

But Brutus says he was ambitious,

And Brutus is an honourable man.

(*Source: Julius Caesar* by William Shakespeare)

For practice

In his novel *Little Dorrit,* Charles Dickens makes fun of officials and bureaucrats who get tied up in form-filling and generate more and more administrative paperwork. He invents an imaginary government department that has turned the creation of unnecessary 'red tape' into an art form and calls it the 'Circumlocution Office' (look back at page 45 to see why Dickens chose this title).

Questions

Read through the following extract.

Choose three examples of irony that you think are particularly effective, and try to explain why you have chosen them.

You could do this exercise either orally or in writing.

The Circumlocution Office was (as everybody knows without being told) the most important Department under Government. No public business of any kind could possibly be done at any time, without the acquiescence of the Circumlocution Office. If another Gunpowder Plot had been discovered half an hour before the lighting of the match, nobody would have been justified in saving the parliament until there had been half a score of boards, half a bushel of minutes, several sacks of official memoranda, and a family-vault full of ungrammatical correspondence, on the part of the Circumlocution Office.

This glorious establishment had been early in the field, when the one sublime principle involving the difficult art of governing a country, was first distinctly revealed to statesmen. It had been foremost to study that bright revelation, and to carry its shining influence through the whole of the official proceedings. Whatever was required to be done, the Circumlocution Office was beforehand with all the public departments in the art of perceiving – HOW NOT TO DO IT.

Through this delicate perception, through the tact with which it invariably seized it, and through the genius with which it always acted on it, the Circumlocution Office had risen to overtop all the public departments…

(*Source: Little Dorrit* by Charles Dickens)

Focus on emotive language

For certain purposes, for example in protesting against a perceived grievance or outrage, an **emotive tone** is often adopted by a writer. As the name implies, this aims at stirring up feelings such as indignation, pity or apprehension in the reader. This effect is achieved by using words or expressions denoting extremes of language.

Typical techniques used in emotive writing include:

- hyperbole
- words denoting powerful sensations and emotions
- many adjectives and adverbs
- vivid imagery (simile and metaphor)
- a dramatic and emotional tone
- anecdotes likely to arouse emotion
- striking sentence structure patterns (see pages 25–27), such as inversion, rhetorical questions, repetition and short sentences.

For practice

The following example was written by a sports journalist criticising the tension at a Glasgow football match:

> Nowhere else on the planet do footballers perform in front of vast crowds so full of bile, hatred and bigotry. I have yet to find another place on the planet where a sporting occasion includes a ritual singing of some ditty celebrating a distant battle which took place over 300 years ago.
>
> (*Source: The Mail on Sunday*)

Here the writer begins with inversion, so that he starts with a strong negative phrase: 'Nowhere else on the planet'. His repetition of 'on the planet' stresses the uniqueness of the situation. He uses words expressing extremes – 'vast', 'full of' – and strong emotions – 'bile, hatred and bigotry'. The effect is one of hyperbole rather than literal truth. He uses so-called loaded words, for example 'some ditty' conveys a tone of contempt.

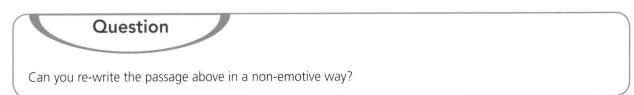

Question

Can you re-write the passage above in a non-emotive way?

This is the opening of a newspaper article in which journalist Andrew Malone reports on Prince William's campaign to save the African rhino.

Question

Can you pick out the ways in which the writer uses emotive language to engage the reader's interest? Try to find one or more examples of each of the techniques listed above.

William's war on the rhino butchers: How the Prince is entering the fray in a dramatic intervention on behalf of the beleaguered animal

The animal was heavily pregnant. But her swollen abdomen did not deter the poachers eyeing her from a position downwind. As this magnificent 28-year-old rhino foraged in the African bush, the men stalking her opened fire.

Death did not come quickly for their prey. Instead, after heavy-calibre bullets ripped into her hide, the wounded animal rampaged off through the bush. The poachers gave chase and, as would become appallingly clear, managed to run the animal to ground.

The creature was still alive when she was eventually found by game rangers in South Africa late last year. But her horn had been hacked from her skull with a machete, leaving a suppurating open wound.

The rangers swiftly put the hideously disfigured animal down and, when they carried out an autopsy, removed the body of an almost perfectly formed baby rhino whose birth had been imminent.

Such harrowing incidents are no longer rare: another six animals were found butchered a few days ago in South Africa's Kruger National Park, riddled with bullets from automatic weapons, their horns cut from their skulls.

In what is being branded the genocide of the rhino, these creatures are being mown down at the rate of more than three a day, fuelled by soaring demand from China and Vietnam, where rhino horn is prized for its supposed medicinal properties. It is now more valuable per ounce than gold, heroin or cocaine.

(*Source:* Andrew Malone, *Daily Mail*)

FURTHER PRACTICE

The following extracts all express a distinctive **tone**.

Tones

a) light-hearted; informal; humorous; chatty; informative
b) reflective; formal; intellectual; thoughtful
c) emotive; angry; emotional; personal
d) impersonal; formal; factual, discursive, balanced and impartial
e) personal; humorous; conversational; informal; rueful
f) rhetorical; impassioned; inspiring; positive
g) ironic; sarcastic, mocking; scathing

Questions

1. Match the tone of each extract with one of the descriptions of tone in the list above. Each of the seven passages is an example of one of these.
2. Give two or three pieces of evidence to justify your choices in question 1.
   Comment on any relevant language features that reinforce the tone, such as: repetition; sentence structure; word choice; use of pronouns; use of imagery; use of abbreviations, slang and informal expressions; hyperbole; emotive language; use of figures and statistics, and so on.

Remember

A question on tone is asking you what the writer's choice of words reveals about his *feelings* or his *attitude* to his subject.

1. (*The closing words of a speech by Hillary Clinton on receiving an honorary degree from St Andrews University. The occasion was the 600th anniversary of the University.*)

   We did just mark the 50th anniversary of Dr King's march on Washington. And I was thinking about how today we need even to expand his very moving aspirational words. We need not only to judge one another by the content of our character, but by the content of our minds and our hearts. Universities like this one bear a special responsibility. In his inaugural address as Rector in 1867, John Stewart Mill said that the university exists for the purpose of laying open to each succeeding generation the accumulated treasures of the thoughts of mankind. And he told students later that day, 'You and your like are the hope and resource of your country in the coming generations.'

   I would only slightly edit those words to say that you and your like are the hope and resource of our world in the coming generations. We look to you to help shape the ideas that will address the great challenges of our time; ideas that will originate in your libraries, in your laboratories, in your conversations, in your debates.

   →

We look for you to be part of a great movement of young people across our world who will not settle for the lowest common denominator, who will not give up your right to be heard, who will not take the easy path of conventional agreement with ideas and policies that are neither founded on evidence nor common sense. We need you to be in a new vanguard for the kind of changes that we are seeking that will make a difference in this world; this networked world where we know more about what goes on everywhere than we used to know about what went on next door.

We cannot succeed without great institutions like St Andrews continuing to speak out, to break barriers; and we cannot succeed without young people who are willing to walk through those openings and help chart a new path for us all. So on behalf of all of my colleagues who have been so honoured today, we regret we could not have been with you on the 500th anniversary but we are delighted to have been with you on the 600th.

We thank you for this great honour but we also leave behind our hope and a challenge that in the years ahead St Andrews will continue to be a place of learning, a place of ferment, a place of excitement that will be looked back on in years to come as one of the engines of the kind of changes our young people, our world, so richly deserve.

(*Source:* Hillary Clinton, 13 September 2013)

2. It always seems, looking at contemporary accounts, as though servants were appallingly badly paid. The earliest records of wages at Castle Howard show that the highest-paid member of the household was the cook, at £36 per year, while the groom, the footmen and the under-butler earned no more than £6 a year – and all of these were deemed 'upper' servants, with related status.

    But these figures are misleading. All the upper servants came into daily contact with the castle guests and would thereby have earned a great deal more than their salaries in tips. Moreover, although the actual wages were so meagre, all expenses were paid, including clothes; in fact a servant's clothes often cost his employer more than his salary. Those servants who did not qualify for a uniform or livery were compensated by a special allowance for clothes.

    Finally, it must be remembered that the servants, particularly the more important ones, lived extremely well. There is a record which shows that eight dozen bottles of port were consumed in the steward's room in a single month during the nineteenth century. The furnishings of the room evoke a comfortable gentlemen's club: leather chairs, a walnut chest, an oval dining-table, two carved gilt wall sconces, and forty-nine prints on the walls. The housekeeper lived in equal splendour with her own suite of rooms.

(*Source: Castle Howard* by Venetia Murray)

3. Enjoying a walk through the park with my husband and children the other week, it felt good to be out with my family in the fresh air. That was until an unleashed dog decided to bound over and gate-crash the outing. Such was this hairy beast's enthusiasm to join our party, he hurtled at my four children like a bowling ball into a line of skittles, and in the process nearly knocked my three-year-old off her feet.

    The hound clearly couldn't understand the fuss as I scooped up my trembling daughter and tried to soothe her tears. But worse still, neither could its owner. Indeed, instead of enquiring if any harm had been done, she threw her mongrel a smile of absolution and excused the excitable hound's behaviour as youthful exuberance. With breath-taking indifference to my traumatised child, she assured us that her thumping great pet 'didn't mean any harm'. And with that, she clicked her mouth, swung the animal's redundant lead round her shoulder and walked off.

➡

Incidents such as this do more than confirm my dislike of dogs. They inflame my loathing for their owners. This dreadful strain of humanity is a breed apart. Marked by a delusional acceptance of anything their pets do, dog owners have transformed turning a blind eye into an Olympic sport. Worse still, their intolerable, sanctimonious conduct means that the rest of us pay the price for their relentless indulgence. But before all those pet-loving detractors start clamouring that I'm over-reacting, my experience last week was no one-off. I could list countless occasions when this kind of thing has happened.

(*Source:* Angela Epstein, *Daily Mail*)

4. When I was 18, my parents were so keen to get rid of me that they presented me with a matching set of steamer trunks and suitcases. You'd have thought they were about to wave me off to New Zealand or India or some remote part of the Empire, the amount of luggage I was smilingly given. In fact, I went to St Andrews University, 12 hours by train from my home in South Wales, and upon disembarking, my grown-up life commenced. In the space of a single railway journey in 1978, I went from being a dependent teenager to an adult, having to fend for myself. And I never looked back.

    Fast forward a quarter of a century, and today's nippers, even if they leave home, keep coming back. My own three sons, aged 27, 24 and 21, are perfect examples of these failed fledglings or 'boomerang children', as they have been called. They've dipped their toes in the waters of the real world, and have all come scurrying back. They're certainly not alone in choosing to remain at home: figures show that a record one-in-three men aged 20 to 34 still live with their parents. A professor at the University of Kent, Frank Furedi, says that 'parents molly-coddling their children' are to blame for this 'boomerang' generation.

    I agree. And, M'lud, I am guilty as charged. With my sons, it began as soon as they were born, with endless treats. As a parent I was far too nice. My own mother and father were remote and Victorian. Adults were people who commanded respect and fear. I'd never have dreamt of being on first-name terms with them. Not now – now everyone is pals.

    I deluged my sons with toys and videos. I took them with me on business trips abroad, enjoying their company. What I'd hoped was that by giving my children a great childhood, they'd have a rich (in experience) launching pad from which to shoot off into grown-up life.

    I hadn't expected any one of them to take a look at grown-up life and think: 'Steady on, I'm not going there.' But that's exactly what all three of them have done. While they all left home in their late teens – two of them for university and one to join the circus – they've all flown back to the nest.

    To be fair, it is a very nice nest. Sadly, rather than being Lord of the Manor, I awoke one day to discover that, with three grown-up sons at home, I'd turned into the janitor-come-chambermaid. I could also be a professional laundryman. Eight loads a weekend is my average. While my now very large boys are only too happy to take up residence in their childhood bedrooms, this extended adolescence is hell for us, their parents.

(*Source:* Roger Lewis, *Daily Mail*)

5. One of the losses modern society feels most keenly is that of a sense of community. We tend to imagine that there once existed a degree of neighbourliness that has been replaced by ruthless anonymity, a state where people pursue contact with one another primarily for restricted, individualistic ends: for financial gain, social advancement or romantic love.

    Some of our nostalgia centres around our reluctance to give charitably to others in distress, but we are as likely to be concerned with pettier symptoms of social separation,

➡

→

our failure to say hello to one another in the street, for instance, or to help elderly neighbours with the shopping. Living in gargantuan cities, we tend to be imprisoned within tribal ghettos based on education, class and profession and may come to view the rest of humanity as an enemy rather than as a sympathetic collective we would aspire to join. It can be extraordinary and odd to start an impromptu conversation with an unknown person in a public space. Once we are past the age of thirty, it is even somewhat surprising to make a new friend.

(*Source: Religion for Atheists* by Alain de Botton)

6. Realism, eh? Courb-et. Mill-et. Man-et. Telling it like it was.

Modern painting starts here. Or that's what they say. The 1850s and '60s saw the French artistic applecart overturned more than once by Gustave Courbet, Jean-Francois Millet and Edouard Manet. Their crime? They dared to paint such unworthy subjects as real people doing everyday things. Why and how? Like much in art, it was a young-blood reaction to an established but outmoded style. No more heavyweight classical allusions for these gents.

'Getting real' put the noses of newspaper critics out of joint. This was the era (sometimes quite like our own), when journals printed detailed, florid descriptions of salon paintings with high-brow or moral content. Paintings whose subjects were (deep breath) Peasants … or Prostitutes … or Death were just asking for trouble. Gus slapped the pundits' faces when he showed his vast *Burial at Ornans* with its real, boring people, its animals and drunken priests. The low-life gathered in his *The Painter's Studio* left everyone speechless. Plus he often used a palette knife. It just wasn't done.

The problem didn't go away. Poor Millet was branded a red-hot momma for several oils showing peasants at work. Much more rumpus was caused by the energetic canvases of Edward Manet. For many they were just about the last straw.

Until the 1870s Manet's technique was based on the opposition of light and shade. Forget subtle sfumato; Manet used Black!! (*Quel horreur!* So what if he'd studied Goya and Velasquez?) But in 1863 things got nasty. M. dared to defy social convention, by showing gratuitous nudity in *Le Dejeuner sur l'Herbe* and *Olympia*. Public decency … family values … morals … the sniping went on for years.

(*Source: Art* by Julian Freeman)

7. (*From the letters page of the* Daily Mail.)

How shameful that the poor staff on the sixth and seventh floors at the BBC's Broadcasting House have been forced to work in an office environment that 'didn't feel like a creative space' and 'wasn't inspiring enough'.

Thankfully, these creative wastelands are to be the subject of a big budget makeover, ripping out the décor that had been part of the £1 billion building when it was opened just 18 months ago. In their place will be an EastEnders-inspired, Albert Square-themed area with iron railings around it, a meeting room named after the Queen Vic pub, and 'street-scape art' featuring landmarks from the soap.

Perhaps, while they're at it, they might dispense with some of the uninspiring 'repeat' programmes these victims of creativity deprivation have been dishing out under the guise of entertainment and education.

Creativity and inspiration do not rely on new carpets and curtains or a replica Queen Vic meeting room – they're about talent, and that's something that doesn't come with the décor.

Other TV channels rely on viewing figures for their economic survival while the BBC has no such motivation and incentive. We simply hand it bucket-loads of cash to spend as it will and worry about the lack of inspiration in the furnishings.

III EVALUATION AND COMPARISON
EVALUATION

Evaluation questions expect you to express a view or come to a judgement of your own on the effect of the language and/or ideas of passages of writing.

Sometimes the questions will begin with the word 'evaluate', and you can also look for clues in the wording of the question. For example,

> To what extent does the writer convince you that...?

This means that you can look at both sides: to some extent the writer may convince you and to some extent he or she may not. You can agree completely that the writer convinces the reader; you can agree that in some ways he or she does and in other ways he or she does not; in theory, you could disagree completely, though in practice there is likely to be more evidence that the argument is convincing than otherwise.

A common question of this type is:

> How effective do you find the last paragraph/sentence as a conclusion to the whole passage?

You can prepare for this in advance by looking out for the following aspects that might make a conclusion 'effective':

- It summarises the arguments of the passage.

- It refers back to points mentioned earlier.

- It picks up on an image mentioned earlier and provides a variation on this.

- It returns to the point the passage started with, giving the passage a circular movement or a sense of completeness.

- It answers a question raised earlier.

- It has a contrasting tone (for example, the writer may adopt a serious tone after using a largely light-hearted or humorous tone in the rest of the passage).

- It leaves the reader thinking what his/her own answer might be (by, for instance, using a rhetorical question).

- It adds impact to the whole passage through techniques of style (e.g. short sentences, questions, puns, exclamations, direct appeals to the reader, humour).

Remember

Be precise! It is important that you give a brief summary of the writer's point each time, providing examples and quotations as necessary. Don't be vague!

Be in proportion! As usual, you should tailor your comments to the number of marks available: for example, by clearly developing a minimum of three separate points if the question is worth 3 marks.

Here is a list of phrases you may find useful in evaluating a conclusion:

- Sums up the arguments in lines…
- Links back to the idea of…
- Returns to the point made earlier that…
- Ends by reasserting…
- Concludes by repeating that…
- Returns to an argument already discussed that…
- Repeats an idea already explored in lines…
- Provides an effective contrast in tone by…
- Provokes the reader to reflect that…

Your answer must show that you understand the *purpose* of a conclusion – that it will:

- sum up the ideas/arguments explored in the rest of the passage
- resolve the arguments in a satisfactory manner, either by stating a definite opinion or leaving this open to the reader
- relate in style or tone (similar or contrasting) to the rest of the passage
- be written in a style that is likely to have an impact on the reader.

Even if the question is only worth a few marks, it can be helpful to make a brief plan first as it will be necessary for you to scan back quickly through the whole of the rest of the article before commenting on the conclusion. There is no need to make your plan neat or legible – only you will read it, so it is best to do it as quickly as possible. Your plan might adopt the following template:

Feature or idea made in conclusion	Links back to…

A fully worked example of a plan is given on page 62.

For practice

The passage that follows comes from the book *Battle Hymn of the Tiger Mother* by Amy Chua, an American of Chinese heritage who is a Professor of Law at Harvard University.

Amy Chua

When a longer extract was published in the *New York Times* it caused a sensation, as her method of bringing up children was so different from the liberal model that had become the norm in America over the previous few decades.

The term 'tiger mother' is now included in the dictionary to mean a very stern, controlling parent who drives her children to succeed. 'Tiger' is used by analogy with 'tiger economy' (which refers to Far Eastern countries such as China and Malaysia), as well as referencing the animal renowned for its ferocity.

It had already been observed that Chinese American children were extremely successful academically compared with the population in America as a whole, a phenomenon that Chua explores and seeks to explain in her book. Her book begins with a list of typical activities that most American parents encourage but which Amy Chua had forbidden her children to do.

[People] wonder what these parents do to produce so many math whizzes and music prodigies, what it's like inside the family, and whether they could do it too. Well, I can tell them, because I've done it. Here are some things my daughters, Sophia and Louisa, were never allowed to do:

- attend a sleepover

- have a playdate

- be in a school play

- complain about not being in a school play

- watch TV or play computer games

- choose their own extracurricular activities

- get any grade less than an A

- not be the No. 1 student in every subject except gym and drama

- play any instrument other than the piano or violin

- not play the piano or violin.

(*Source: Battle Hymn of the Tiger Mother by Amy Chua*)

For discussion

Discuss your thoughts on this list of banned activities and the consequences of enforcing the ban.

The following exercises are designed to provide practice in evaluation questions. You may go directly to these exercises, or you may begin by completing the full set of questions, which is to be found in Appendix II (page 107).

Passage 1

Tiger Mother

What Chinese parents understand is that nothing is fun until you're good at it. To get good at anything you have to work, and children on their own never want to work, which is why it is crucial to override their preferences. This often requires fortitude on the part of the parents because the child will resist; things are always hardest at the
5   beginning, which is where Western parents tend to give up. But if done properly, the Chinese strategy produces a virtuous circle. Tenacious practice, practice, practice is crucial for excellence; rote repetition is underrated in America. Once a child starts to excel at something – whether it's math, piano, pitching or ballet – he or she gets praise, admiration and satisfaction. This builds confidence and makes the once not-fun activity
10   fun. This in turn makes it easier for the parent to get the child to work even more.

Chinese parents can get away with things that Western parents can't. Once when I was young – maybe more than once – when I was extremely disrespectful to my mother, my father angrily called me 'garbage' in our native Hokkien dialect. It worked really well. I felt terrible and deeply ashamed of what I had done. But it didn't damage my self-esteem
15   or anything like that. I knew exactly how highly he thought of me. I didn't actually think

→

I was worthless or feel like a piece of garbage. As an adult, I once did the same thing to my daughter Sophia, calling her garbage in English when she acted extremely disrespectfully toward me. When I mentioned at a dinner party that I had done this, I was immediately ostracized. One guest got so upset she broke down in tears and had to leave early.

20 Chinese parents can order their kids to get straight A's. Western parents can only ask their kids to try their best. Chinese parents can say, 'You're lazy. All your classmates are getting ahead of you.' By contrast, Western parents have to struggle with their own conflicted feelings about achievement, and try to persuade themselves that they're not disappointed about how their kids turned out.

25 I've thought long and hard about how Chinese parents can get away with what they do. I think there are three big differences between the Chinese and Western parental mind-sets.

First, I've noticed that Western parents are extremely anxious about their children's self-esteem. They worry about how their children will feel if they fail at something, and they constantly try to reassure their children about how good they are, notwithstanding
30 a mediocre performance on a test or at a recital. In other words, Western parents are concerned about their children's psyches. Chinese parents aren't. They assume strength, not fragility, and as a result they behave very differently. For example, if a child comes home with an A-minus on a test, a Western parent will most likely praise the child. The Chinese mother will gasp in horror and ask what went wrong. Chinese parents demand
35 perfect grades because they believe that their child can get them. If their child doesn't get them, the Chinese parent assumes it's because the child didn't work hard enough. That's why the solution to substandard performance is always to excoriate, punish and shame the child. The Chinese parent believes that their child will be strong enough to take the shaming and to improve from it. (And when Chinese kids do excel, there is plenty of ego-
40 inflating parental praise lavished in the privacy of the home.)

Second, Chinese parents believe that their kids owe them everything. The reason for this is a little unclear, but it's probably a combination of Confucian* filial piety and the fact that the parents have sacrificed and done so much for their children. (And it's true that Chinese mothers get in the trenches, putting in long gruelling hours personally tutoring, training,
45 interrogating and spying on their kids.) Anyway, the understanding is that Chinese children must spend their lives repaying their parents by obeying them and making them proud.

By contrast, I don't think most Westerners have the same view of children being permanently indebted to their parents. My husband actually has the opposite view. 'Children don't choose their parents,' he once said to me. 'They don't even choose to be
50 born. It's parents who foist life on their kids, so it's the parents' responsibility to provide for them. Kids don't owe their parents anything. Their duty will be to their own kids.' This strikes me as a terrible deal for the Western parent.

Third, Chinese parents believe that they know what is best for their children and therefore override all of their children's own desires and preferences. That's why Chinese daughters
55 can't have boyfriends in high school and why Chinese kids can't go to sleepaway camp. It's also why no Chinese kid would ever dare say to their mother, 'I got a part in the school play! I'm Villager Number Six. I'll have to stay after school for rehearsal every day from 3:00 to 7:00, and I'll also need a ride on weekends.' God help any Chinese kid who tried that one.

Don't get me wrong: it's not that Chinese parents don't care about their children. Just
60 the opposite. They would give up anything for their children. It's just an entirely different parenting model.

* Confucian: Relating to the ideas of Confucius, a Chinese philosopher.

(*Source: Battle Hymn of the Tiger Mother* by Amy Chua)

Question

Evaluate the effectiveness of the final paragraph as a conclusion to the passage as a whole.

(3 marks)

Specimen plan

In the exam, you will have to do the whole plan yourself. Here, the first part of the plan is done for you. Complete the 'Links back to…' part of the plan, and then answer the question in sentences.

Feature or idea made in conclusion	Links back to…
'Don't get me wrong' – humble, pleading tone, wanting readers to be on her side.	Contrasts effectively with earlier tone which was … when she said…
'It's not that Chinese parents don't care' – plea that the harsh regime has a loving basis.	Repeats her earlier assertion that…
Two short sentences, one a minor sentence, 'Just … children'.	Simplicity of sentence structure and wording creates tone of … which emphasises…
'just an entirely different parenting model' – conciliatory tone, acknowledges that Chinese model is just one style, and that others may be valid.	This is likely to mollify the reader as it softens the apparently critical tone of her earlier comments, which seemed to suggest…

The final answer can be written in a paragraph or laid out in bullet-point form.

COMPARISON

The final question in the Reading for Understanding, Analysis and Evaluation paper will ask you to make a comparison with another passage on the same topic. All you are asked to do is to read through the second passage, noting similarities and differences with the first one.

You must then answer the question that follows, which will ask you to compare and/or contrast the two passages. The instructions say you may answer this question in continuous prose or in a series of developed bullet points.

Read through Passage 2 below, and think about the key areas in which it compares and contrasts with Passage 1.

Passage 2

In this article, Jemima Lewis reflects on how she brings up her own children and also evaluates the criticism of more 'pushy' parenting styles.

Are you a 'pushy parent'? Do you spend your afternoons ferrying children between Mandarin lessons and taekwondo? Make them practise their piano scales until their fingers throb? Run up and down the football touchline barking out instructions?

5 Nope, nor me. And here's the mysterious thing: I don't know anybody who does. Not a single soul. Deeply immersed though I am in the world of middle-class parenting – my three flaxen-haired, Breton-topped children couldn't look more like a Mini Boden[1] catalogue if you ironed them flat and slipped them through the letterbox – this whole 'pushy' thing seems to have passed me by.

My children – like most of the children I know – watch a bit too much telly for their own
10 good. Their teeth are not always as clean as they might be. Their manners are variable, at best, and their accomplishments limited by the fact that I am too tired and busy to take them to any after-school clubs.

How did I achieve this zen-like state of lazy parenting? Partly, perhaps, it's a matter of context. My children go to a state school in east London. By the sounds of things, private
15 school parents are pushier – and no wonder. School fees are so expensive that you have to be super-rich or heroically self-sacrificing to go private. Either way, expectations will be high.

The current edition of *Attain*, the journal of the Independent Association of Prep Schools (IAPS), contains two articles from head teachers despairing at the excesses of competitive parents.

20 Leonard Blom, headmaster of St Aubyn's preparatory school in London, reports that some parents are destroying their children's enjoyment of sport by screaming 'hysterically' at them from the sidelines. Mr Blom describes how one father got so carried away while watching a junior rugby game that he ran on to the pitch and took a line-out himself; while a mother collapsed from exhaustion after pacing alongside a swimming
25 pool during a race, shouting at her daughter.

[1] Boden: up-market mail order clothing company whose catalogue features photographs of beautiful child models

➜

➡️

Meanwhile Julie Robinson, a former headmistress who now works for the IAPS (Independent Association of Prep Schools) warns that 'overbearing parents' are making their children stressed and anxious by not giving them any free time in which to be bored. 'It is all too easy,' she says, 'for parents to be sucked into a competitive busyness,
30 ensuring that children are constantly occupied and stimulated.'

Boo hiss to them! What satisfactory baddies they make, these rich neurotics, ruining their children's lives by driving them too hard. We don't even have to qualify our disapproval with pity, the way we do when disapproving of poor parents.

There are now two types of bogeyman in modern parenting, occupying opposite poles.
35 At one end, the negligent or abusive parent: a slack-jawed troglodyte from the primeval swamps of the underclass. At the other, the pushy parent: the gimlet-eyed Lady Macbeth of the nursery.

The territory in between – where we are allowed to just get on with being parents, however inexpertly – seems to get narrower all the time. And we parents collude in our
40 own entrapment. The pleasure we lazy ones take in censuring our pushier brethren is, in fact, just another form of competition. It makes us feel better about our own inadequacies.

A father who gets over-excited on the touchline may be embarrassing, but at least he is there. Driving your child from Kumon class to karate lesson might not seem like an
45 expression of love, but it is one. Perhaps the real reason I can't see any 'pushy parents' among my friends is that they are actual people, not fairy-tale villains.

(*Source:* Jemima Lewis, *Daily Telegraph*)

Question

Both passages look at the topic of bringing up children. Identify key areas where Jemima Lewis agrees or disagrees with Amy Chua.
You may answer this question in continuous prose or in a series of developed bullet points.   **(5 marks)**

Again, the best way to approach this question is to make a brief plan. One or two points have been put in to get you started.

Area of Disagreement	Passage 1	Passage 2
How strict the writer is as a parent	Chua admits to being very strict and forcing her children to work hard	Lewis has a more relaxed attitude to parenting. She lets her children watch too much television, for example
Areas of Agreement	**Passage 1**	**Passage 2**
Belief that pushing children is actually evidence of love	Chua maintains Chinese parents care about their children: 'they would give up anything for their children'	Lewis accepts that pushing children to achieve is a form of love: the 'over-excited father… may be embarrassing, but at least he is there.' Spending time driving children to classes and extra-curricular activities is 'an expression of love'

For discussion

Read the paragraph below, which was the conclusion of an article looking at the pros and cons of parental 'pushing'. How far do you feel it vindicates Amy Chua's views?

Research into 'pushy parenting' is inconclusive. One study published recently found British children were well behind students in the Far East in science, maths and reading. After interviewing head teachers, the report's authors said children whose parents have higher expectations perform better.

Another report, however, criticised parents for seeing their children as extensions of themselves.

(*Source:* James Edgar, *Daily Telegraph*)

PART TWO: APPLYING THE SKILLS

In this section you will find four newspaper articles with attached questions. These passages are designed to provide an intermediate stage in applying the skills you will have to use in the Reading for Understanding, Analysis and Evaluation paper.

There is an emphasis on technical terms so that you can become thoroughly familiar with their use. These are all explained in the Reading Skills section of the book.

Most of the practice questions are fairly short. In the exam, however, there will also be longer questions worth 3, 4 or 5 marks.

The source of the texts

Regular reading of quality journalism is one of the best ways of preparing for the Higher English Reading for Understanding, Analysis and Evaluation paper as most of the passages used in this section of the exam are drawn from newspaper sources.

We're not talking about the news reports on the front pages or the sports reports at the back. The most useful passages are editorials and feature articles.

- Papers like *The Times*, the *Daily Telegraph*, the *Guardian*, *The Herald* and *The Scotsman* will have a column, headed with the newspaper's logo, usually containing three short articles giving the paper's opinion on the main issues of the day.

- Feature articles will focus in more detail on a controversial issue and may be written by an outside expert rather than one of the newspaper's own staff. Articles of this kind are similar to the discursive writing element of your folio.

How to analyse a newspaper article

Once you have discussed one or two of the passages below, it would be useful to go to newspaper sources and cut out examples of similar articles, or download them from the paper's website. These articles could then be used as the basis for class discussion.

Here is a convenient checklist of what to look for:

Content
- How does the writer grab the reader's attention in the opening sentence or headline?
- Are there any clues in the introductory paragraph that suggest how the rest of the article will develop?
- Does the writer use topic sentences to introduce his or her points?
- What kind of evidence is used to back-up the argument (e.g. statistics, quotations, pieces of factual information)?
- Can you summarise the passage by identifying one main point per paragraph?
- How effectively does the last paragraph draw the article to a conclusion?

Style, expression and tone

- Does the writer adopt an objective (i.e. unbiased) or subjective (i.e. personal) approach? Can you identify examples of word choice that make this clear?
- Is the style formal or informal, or is there a mixture of different registers? Can you identify expressions that show this?
- Does the writer use emotive language to convey how strongly he or she feels? Can you identify examples of emotive word choice?
- Are you aware of any particular tone (e.g. humorous, ironic, sarcastic, serious)? Can you identify examples of word choice that make this clear?
- Do you notice any particularly effective uses of sentence structure? If so, how do these help to reinforce the argument?
- Are there any examples of figurative language? What is the effect of it?
- Does the writer use any other literary techniques that you have studied in the course of this book?

FOCUS ON READING 1

Football Results

The time is long past when missing Saturday night TV results would leave you bereft, writes Graeme Macpherson.

a) What is the one main point that the writer is making in this paragraph? **(2 marks)**

b) What sentence structure techniques does he use to make this a particularly effective opening paragraph? **(4 marks)**

c) Explain how the first sentence of paragraph 2 acts as a **topic sentence** for the rest of the paragraph. **(2 marks)**

d) Explain how the first sentence of paragraph 3 performs a **linking function**. **(2 marks)**

e) '…finding out the scores on Saturday evening … was a tricky business'. How does the writer develop this point in paragraphs 4, 5 and 6? **(3 marks)**

1. If you don't want to know the score… well, pack up your things and move to an uninhabited island somewhere in the South Pacific. It's your only hope. And even then someone would probably still row ashore uninvited with a laptop, access to a WiFi signal and Twitter feed, and start reading out football results like some sort of annoying hybrid of James Alexander Gordon* and Captain James Cook**.

2. Knowledge these days is instant. If a goal is scored in any league, in any country, at just about any level, then chances are someone will be there to report on it, spreading the news far and wide on television, radio and the all-seeing eye that is the internet. Football hipsters sure have it easy in the modern era.

3. Of course, it wasn't always so. Those of us old enough to remember when a mobile phone meant stretching the cable of your landline to see if you could reach the next room, can recall a time when finding out the scores on Saturday evening (and it was always a Saturday evening) was a tricky business.

4. Even if you were at a match it wasn't always straightforward, with some clubs like Dundee United putting results next to random letters on their scoreboard in the hope that you would buy their match programme to discover just what the heck it all meant.

5. The alternative was to get yourself in front of a television at the appropriate moment. Thus did sales assistants at Arnotts, Frasers and other sizeable department stores observe that the number of people seemingly interested in buying a new TV would spike every Saturday evening around 4:45 p.m. Similarly, the drop-off rate would be just as dramatic once the results had been read out and the final credits started rolling to signal the end of *Grandstand*.

* Until the early 1990s, James Alexander Gordon was well-known as a radio announcer who used to read out football results.
** Captain James Cook was an eighteenth-century naval captain and explorer. He is the first known European to make contact with the eastern coastline of Australia and the Hawaiian Islands.

f) How does the writer's word choice in paragraph 6 emphasise how anxious football fans were to find out the results? **(3 marks)**

6. There won't be a football fan alive of a certain vintage who, upon finding themselves in town around full-time on a Saturday, hasn't at one point instantly dropped whatever they were doing and run towards the nearest available shop that might have a television in the window. If you were too late, and none of your friends or family knew the scores either, then that was probably you stuck wondering until the next morning when you would dash out frantically to get the Sunday papers.

g) In your own words, explain the main point the writer is making in paragraph 7. (Do not refer to the specific examples given.) **(2 marks)**

7. At least those in the country had a few options when it came to learning the weekend's results. Anyone overseas was left with the choice of either making an expensive telephone call home, or waiting patiently until a British newspaper surfaced somewhere in the coming days. As a poor student living in Germany in the pre-internet era, the second option was usually preferable. It also meant that not hearing for a few days that St Mirren had lost, again, couldn't ruin your weekend.

h) Identify one language feature in paragraph 8 and explain how it helps the reader understand the main point from the previous paragraph. **(3 marks)**

8. The Monday morning expedition – a full 40 hours after full-time – would involve a 10-minute train journey from the student digs into the city centre to the newspaper shop in the main station in the hope that there would be a copy of the *Sunday Mail* or *News of the World* still in stock.

9. Then there would be an as-quick-as-possible flick to the appropriate page, before scanning the scores and trying to commit them all to memory like some sort of deleted scene from *Good Will Hunting*. Then, all the while avoiding eye contact with the shopkeeper, the paper would be returned to the shelf and the reverse journey begun, the week having now begun with either heart-lifting or heart-breaking news, depending on results.

i) Suggest one advantage and one disadvantage of modern technology compared to the way things were in the writer's younger days. **(2 marks)**

10. All of this, of course, will sound positively alien to anyone under 25 who has grown up with every bit of information available to them at the touch of a button, but similarly disadvantaged by the inherent inability to hold conversations with other human beings without the use of an electronic device.

j) Explain how the word choice in the last paragraph shows the writer's personal opinion about modern technology. **(3 marks)**

11. Those who use Twitter for their instant gratification can have minute-by-minute details of the day's major sporting events for 24 hours solid. *The Likely Lads** wouldn't have liked it one bit.

* *The Likely Lads* refers to a TV sitcom first screened in 1964. It dealt with the antics of two young factory workers from north-east England whose main interests were football and girls. A famous episode featured the lads trying to avoid hearing the result of a football match they were going to watch on TV.
(*Source:* Graeme Macpherson, *The Herald*)

Extra question

In your own words, summarise the main point from each paragraph, omitting evidence and examples. Two have been done for you.

Paragraph	Main point
1	There is literally nowhere a person can go to avoid finding out football results.
2	
3	
4	Even spectators who were present at a match found it difficult to follow the score.
5	
6	
7	
8	
9	
10	
11	

FOCUS ON READING 2

The Crombie Coat

In this article, Nick Foulkes, journalist, historian and style expert, discusses the Crombie coat, which was chosen as the uniform for Peter Capaldi in his role as Doctor Who.

a) The writer uses language playfully in this introduction to create **a humorous tone**. Can you find some examples of **alliteration** that illustrate this? **(3 marks)**

b) Explain why the word 'sacred' has a tongue-in-cheek tone when used here. **(2 marks)**

c) The juxtaposition of **formal and informal** language also continues the **playful tone**. Can you find examples to illustrate this contrast? **(2 marks)**

1. I can't help feeling a twinge of envy for the wonderful wardrobe opportunities extended to Peter Capaldi in his role as the latest incarnation of Doctor Who. Viewed from the wardrobe department, the bearers of the sacred sonic screwdriver have proved an interesting bunch: Jon Pertwee captured the neo-Victorian velvet dandyism of early seventies' Britain; Tom Baker's scarf nodded to late hippydom; Peter Davison's panama hat and cricket sweater surfed the Brideshead* nostalgia boom of the early eighties, and so on.

* *Brideshead Revisited*, a TV programme, much of which was set at Oxford University in 1930s.

→

d) In paragraph 2, the writer continues the **mock serious tone**, using high flown, intellectual language. Which word provides a **comic contrast**? **(1 mark)**

e) A 'palimpsest' is a scroll made of parchment or vellum that is reused by having the surface scraped. Explain how this is an effective **metaphor** for the Crombie coat. **(2 marks)**

f) Identify three pieces of evidence that show the Crombie coat has had a distinguished history. Use your own words as far as possible. **(3 marks)**

g) Explain the point made by the anecdote about the phone call in adding to the impression of the coat's qualities. **(2 marks)**

h) Identify the phrase in paragraph 6 that helps you understand the meaning of 'nomenklatura'. **(1 mark)**

i) By referring to at least one example, analyse how the writer's use of imagery is effective in this paragraph. Possible choices are highlighted to help you. **(2 marks)**

2. The defining garment of the Capaldi era will be the Crombie overcoat. As a metaphor for the state of the nation, it is an interesting one, in that it is teamed with a pair of Doc Martens. Mention those two totemic items of clobber to a man of Capaldi's vintage in a word association test and the answer will be 'skinhead'. But the Crombie is as versatile as it is indestructible; a palimpsest upon which successive generations of Britons have written their story. The coat of kings and rude boys alike owes its name to John Crombie, an early nineteenth-century cloth producer. Rather like Woody Allen's *Zelig*, the firm and its products wove themselves into every subsequent era of British history.

3. Crombie was commended at the Great Exhibition of 1851, the event that marked the beginning of the High Victorian era, and it became one of the great British exports of the age of empire. Crombie ran the blockade during the American Civil War to supply the Confederates with their Rebel Grey. During the siege of Paris in 1871 an order of the firm's fabric was floated in by hot air balloon; and by the end of the century the stuff was being shipped to Russia.

4. It was Crombie that gave us the famous 'British Warm' during the First World War when the firm turned itself to the production of military greatcoats, which were built from the tough heavy Melton fabric that has ensured Crombie coats outlive many generations of owners. 'I had a recent phone call from a man,' recalls Alan Lewis, the firm's owner and chairman, 'and he said: "You are chairman of Crombie. I bought my coat in 1948. Would you please change the lining."'

5. Given that these coats wear out their owners rather than the other way around it is probably useful for Lewis that 'we used to sell 50,000 coats into Soviet Russia, and when I went to Russia I asked where the Crombie coats were'. He was told that they were being worn by the nomenklatura; Gorbachev was wearing a Crombie long before he started advertising Louis Vuitton luggage.

6. It says something for the versatility of an overcoat that it can be simultaneously popular with the ruling elite of the Soviet Union and the tribal subcultures of British youth. The Crombie name has a sort of magic that knows no barrier and its appeal is nowhere better summed up than in

→

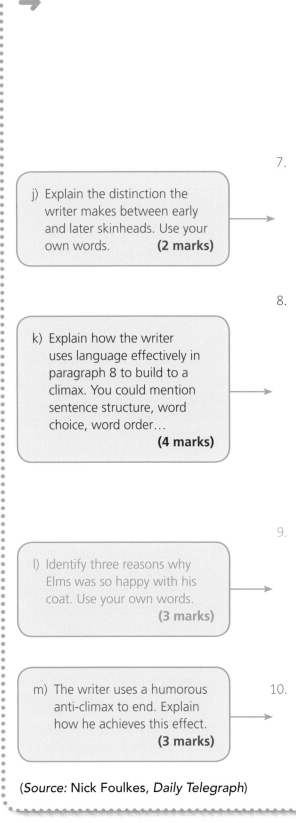

The Way We Wore, Robert Elms's sartorial autobiography. The flattering and forever sharp silhouette of the Crombie, with its fly front, velvet collar and carmine lining, hovers over this book. One of the most moving passages comes when the laureate of late twentieth-century urban style describes the moment of epiphany when he finally slips into his first Crombie.

j) Explain the distinction the writer makes between early and later skinheads. Use your own words. **(2 marks)**

7. Early skinheads were not caricature orcs of the Right, but detail-obsessed descendants of the suited-and-scootered mods of the sixties. As a precocious pre-teen skinhead, young Elms assembled a comprehensive wardrobe, with one notable lacuna: 'I never got a Crombie, not even a snide one off a market stall.'

k) Explain how the writer uses language effectively in paragraph 8 to build to a climax. You could mention sentence structure, word choice, word order… **(4 marks)**

8. He waited almost a quarter of a century until he could wear the real thing. 'I never let go of the idea that there was only one pukka overcoat. Then one day, when I was in my mid-thirties, strolling along Savile Row, planning suits that would never get made, I saw that a certain Crombie and Sons of Aberdeen, Scotland, had opened a new shop of their own and there in the window was the coat. Navy blue, heavy felt wool, fly-fronted, square shoulders, black velvet collar. I was nervous when I walked in. After 24 long years a tiny dream was about to be realised.'

l) Identify three reasons why Elms was so happy with his coat. Use your own words. **(3 marks)**

9. Unlike most childhood ambitions achieved in later life, the coat did not disappoint. Long after the pre-teen skinhead had metamorphosed into a writer, Elms would find himself consulting the label to reassure himself that 'it still spells out the same all-important word. I wear it to football sometimes when it's cold, which makes me smile. It's an excellent coat.'

m) The writer uses a humorous anti-climax to end. Explain how he achieves this effect. **(3 marks)**

10. And what worked for the British Army in the trenches of the First World War, the Politburo atop Lenin's tomb and the chilly terraces of Britain's football grounds is more than equal to the Daleks and Cybermen.

(*Source:* Nick Foulkes, *Daily Telegraph*)

Extra questions

1. What do you think is the main purpose of this article? Is it to inform, to entertain, or to reflect? Explain your reasons for your answer. **(4 marks)**
2. Evaluate the effectiveness of the final paragraph as a conclusion to the whole passage. **(5 marks)**

FOCUS ON READING 3

Scotland in Hollywood

Journalist Jim McBeth reports on a discussion with some Scottish actors of how Scotland and Scottish accents have been depicted in films and TV over the years.

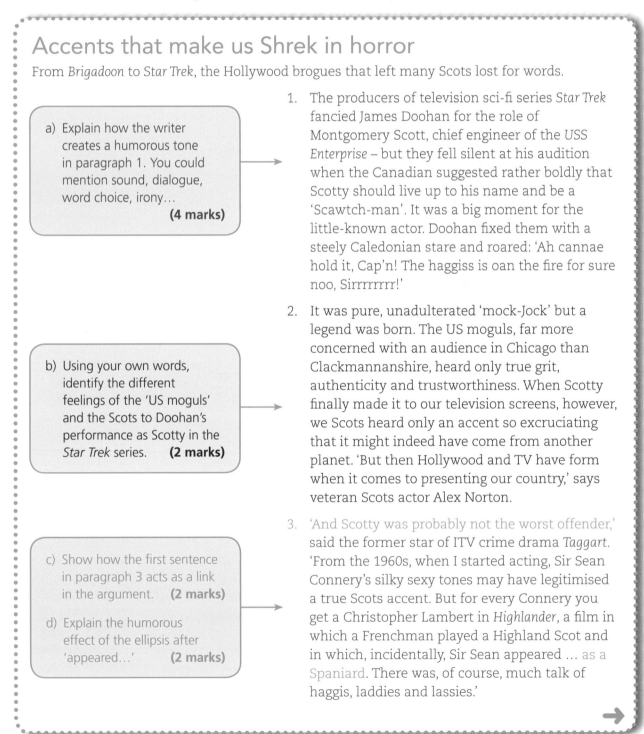

Accents that make us Shrek in horror

From *Brigadoon* to *Star Trek*, the Hollywood brogues that left many Scots lost for words.

a) Explain how the writer creates a humorous tone in paragraph 1. You could mention sound, dialogue, word choice, irony… **(4 marks)**

b) Using your own words, identify the different feelings of the 'US moguls' and the Scots to Doohan's performance as Scotty in the *Star Trek* series. **(2 marks)**

c) Show how the first sentence in paragraph 3 acts as a link in the argument. **(2 marks)**

d) Explain the humorous effect of the ellipsis after 'appeared…' **(2 marks)**

1. The producers of television sci-fi series *Star Trek* fancied James Doohan for the role of Montgomery Scott, chief engineer of the *USS Enterprise* – but they fell silent at his audition when the Canadian suggested rather boldly that Scotty should live up to his name and be a 'Scawtch-man'. It was a big moment for the little-known actor. Doohan fixed them with a steely Caledonian stare and roared: 'Ah cannae hold it, Cap'n! The haggiss is oan the fire for sure noo, Sirrrrrrrr!'

2. It was pure, unadulterated 'mock-Jock' but a legend was born. The US moguls, far more concerned with an audience in Chicago than Clackmannanshire, heard only true grit, authenticity and trustworthiness. When Scotty finally made it to our television screens, however, we Scots heard only an accent so excruciating that it might indeed have come from another planet. 'But then Hollywood and TV have form when it comes to presenting our country,' says veteran Scots actor Alex Norton.

3. 'And Scotty was probably not the worst offender,' said the former star of ITV crime drama *Taggart*. 'From the 1960s, when I started acting, Sir Sean Connery's silky sexy tones may have legitimised a true Scots accent. But for every Connery you get a Christopher Lambert in *Highlander*, a film in which a Frenchman played a Highland Scot and in which, incidentally, Sir Sean appeared … as a Spaniard. There was, of course, much talk of haggis, laddies and lassies.'

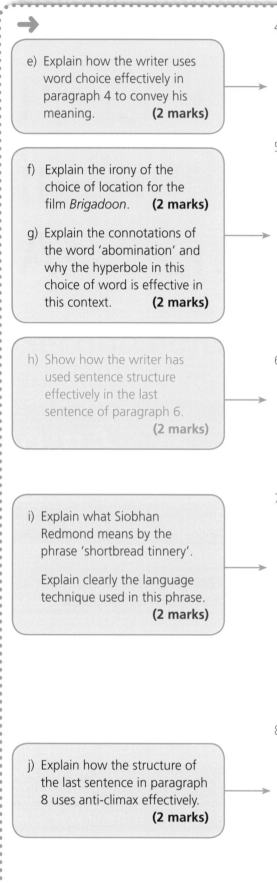

e) Explain how the writer uses word choice effectively in paragraph 4 to convey his meaning. **(2 marks)**

f) Explain the irony of the choice of location for the film *Brigadoon*. **(2 marks)**

g) Explain the connotations of the word 'abomination' and why the hyperbole in this choice of word is effective in this context. **(2 marks)**

h) Show how the writer has used sentence structure effectively in the last sentence of paragraph 6. **(2 marks)**

i) Explain what Siobhan Redmond means by the phrase 'shortbread tinnery'.

Explain clearly the language technique used in this phrase. **(2 marks)**

j) Explain how the structure of the last sentence in paragraph 8 uses anti-climax effectively. **(2 marks)**

4. Hollywood circles demand that a 'Scots' accent be 'ancient, whimsical and charming', which has often led to lilting nonsense or an indecipherable growl, unrecognisable to Scots who, as a result, have spent many an evening cringing in front of the TV or cinema screen.

5. Mr Norton added, '*Brigadoon*, the 1954 film about "Scotland" with Gene Kelly, would have to be a low – a make-believe Scotland with very strange folk dressed in even stranger tartan outfits. Legend has it the film-makers came to Scotland to scout locations – and decided Scotland was not Scottish enough. They built the set on a back lot in Hollywood. I appeared in *Gregory's Girl*, which was re-dubbed with 'posh' voices for the international audience. It was an **abomination** to do that.'

6. 'The notion of Scottishness has often been built around the accents – from the genteel Highlander in *Whisky Galore!* to the fairy-tale accent of *Shrek*, to Forsyth's teenagers and the Glasgow hard men of McDougall's plays. Ever since a Scotsman invented television, television and movies have been inventing Scotsmen.'

7. Glasgow-born actress Siobhan Redmond said: 'People who don't hear our accents all the time genuinely cannot tell the difference between mine, yours and the guy who played Scotty in *Star Trek*.' Miss Redmond points to a sequence in *The Barkleys of Broadway*, the 1949 musical starring Ginger Rogers and Fred Astaire, which features the famous dancing couple as Highlanders. 'It's pure shortbread tinnery,' said the actress. 'But it's an act within an act within an act and hopefully no one believed they spoke like that in the real world.'

8. Mr Norton added, 'Unless you are a genuine Jock, putting on a Scots accent is like doing your own stunts. It's high-risk and can so easily go wrong. One reason it has been strangled is because the true Scots accent is so rarely heard. As a result, Americans are not interested in realism. They want a storybook accent that reflects an ancient land of castles, bagpipes and wee dugs like Greyfriars Bobby.

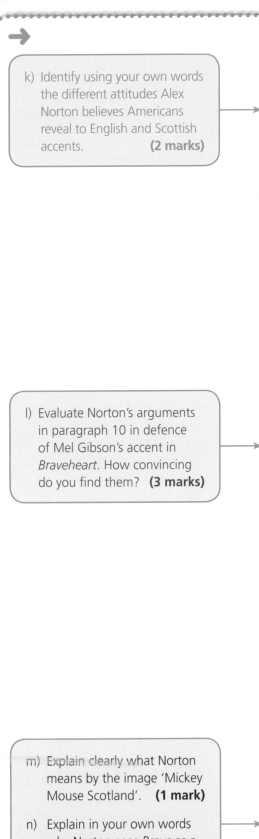

k) Identify using your own words the different attitudes Alex Norton believes Americans reveal to English and Scottish accents. **(2 marks)**

l) Evaluate Norton's arguments in paragraph 10 in defence of Mel Gibson's accent in *Braveheart*. How convincing do you find them? **(3 marks)**

m) Explain clearly what Norton means by the image 'Mickey Mouse Scotland'. **(1 mark)**

n) Explain in your own words why Norton sees *Brave* as a turning point in Hollywood's treatment of Scotland and the Scottish accent. **(2 marks)**

9. 'We should be flattered because they tend to give an English accent to the baddies. We have an underdog accent, humorous and trustworthy. That's why a fantasy character such as Shrek ends up being Scottish. And if you are a Hollywood mogul, you don't care what audiences in Alloa think. You care about people in the American Midwest.'

10. Mr Norton's research unearthed admiration among the acting fraternity for the 'authenticity' of Mel Gibson's Scottish accent in *Braveheart*, the Australian actor and director's epic tale of the thirteenth-century patriot, William Wallace. The film may have inflamed the Scottish psyche when it was released in 1995 but Mr Gibson's accent did come in for a bit of stick. The criticism was unjustified, said Mr Norton, who added, 'It was a pretty standard modern Scottish accent. Who knows what William Wallace would have sounded like? And a story about the life of Wallace would never have been told if someone of the stature of Gibson had not been involved. Good on him, I say. The Scots who appeared with him in that movie were impressed.' *Game of Thrones* star James Cosmo, who played Wallace's right-hand man, was one of them. He said, 'He did a pretty good job. I couldn't fault it.'

11. And while Mr Norton agrees that modern television such as BBC's *Still Game* and films such as Irvine Welsh's *Trainspotting* have done much to present authentic Scottish voices, the actor believes the Disney Corporation has done more than anyone. Mr Norton, who did voice work on *Brave*, the story of the wilful medieval Highland princess Merida, added, 'Disney was meticulous in portraying real Scottish accents and dialects. It was a breakthrough. The involvement of Disney suggested sugary sentimentality and Mickey Mouse Scotland. It was far from it. The Scottish accent and dialects were presented in all their glory without cringe or compromise. It was fantastic. The film was so good that producers reasoned that the audience would "tune in". They were right because it is a nonsense to suggest people outside Scotland cannot understand the accent. As a result of *Brave*, we need not look back. The days of Harry Lauder* are over.'

* Harry Lauder: Stereotypical kilted Scottish entertainer of the early twentieth century.
(*Source:* Jim McBeth, *Daily Mail*)

Extra questions

Look at the title and subtitle of the article.
a) Identify the writer's view of Scots accents in most Hollywood films. **(1 mark)**
b) Explain any one **play on words** in these lines. **(2 marks)**

For discussion

In a class or group, discuss your experiences of how Scotland is portrayed in more recent films and television. Are the days of stereotypes like Harry Lauder really over?

Consider other national stereotypes as they are portrayed in films or TV, for example Germans, French, Irish, Americans and Russians. To what extent do you think they might be offensive?

FOCUS ON READING 4

Apprenticeships

Ellen E. Jones is intrigued to learn that 18-year-olds are to be recruited as apprentice spies. She suggests that apprenticeships in less glamorous areas may be the way forward in solving youth unemployment, in preference to university education.

a) Comment on how the writer uses **sentence structure** to provide an effective opening to the article. **(2 marks)**

b) In your own words, state three qualities that young people have that make them ideal spies. **(3 marks)**

c) How does the writer's use of **language** in paragraph 2 emphasise that spying is now a more technical, IT-based occupation? **(2 marks)**

d) Explain how the writer uses figures effectively to create an **ironic tone** in the last sentence of paragraph 2. **(2 marks)**

e) In your own words, **summarise** the point the writer is making in the second sentence of paragraph 3. **(2 marks)**

f) Using information from paragraph 4, explain how the tasks carried out by spies have changed. Remember to use your own words where possible. **(4 marks)**

1. What are today's politically disengaged, tech-obsessed, dole-scrounging young good for? A career in international espionage, that's what. The Government has announced a two-year apprenticeships scheme that will recruit 18-year-old school leavers as 'trainee spies' for MI5, MI6 and GCHQ*. It might sound like a radical move, but modern spying requires several qualities that the Facebook generation has in abundance: they're tech-savvy, have an apolitical outlook and a complete indifference to the concept of privacy.

2. Israeli PM Benjamin Netanyahu recognised this special aptitude of the young when he announced a cyber-espionage training programme for 'future interceptors for the State of Israel', aged 16–18. China is believed to employ thousands of people in their late teens and twenties in the world's largest institutionalised hacking operation, while the US has just spent $1.5bn on a cybersecurity 'Data Center' in Utah in a bid to keep up. Britain's own spy kids scheme by contrast has only 'dozens' of spaces available, leaving us roughly 964,900 jobs short of a solution to the youth unemployment crisis.

3. One unusual apprenticeship won't change that, but it does point the way to a new approach to tackling youth unemployment. Instead of forcing graduates into non-grad jobs and non-grads into unemployment, perhaps it's time to reassess which jobs really require a university education.

4. Once upon a time in the Cold War, wannabe agents of the British secret services needed only matriculate at Oxbridge, then loiter around the cloister, awaiting their tap on the shoulder. Now that the job involves fewer café assignations with mysterious Russians and more sifting through mountains of ill-gotten computer data, it makes sense that recruitment and training processes change too.

* GCHQ: The Government Communications Headquarters is a British intelligence agency.

g) Show how the first sentence in paragraph 5 has a linking function in the argument. **(2 marks)**

5. Espionage is not the only profession that has changed a lot since the Cold War, and it's not the only profession that should welcome an update to recruitment and training practices either. A well-designed apprenticeship in many careers that are traditionally the preserve of the privileged – politics, journalism, publishing, fashion and film-making, for instance – could provide not only actual on-the-job training and a mapped-out career path, but also many of the other benefits we associate with a university degree.

h) In the first sentence in paragraph 6 the writer uses a financial metaphor to illustrate how students acquire social advantages by attending a good university. Can you identify the words that comprise this metaphor? **(2 marks)**

i) How does the writer use contrast effectively in paragraph 6 to show the reality of working as a spy for MI6? **(2 marks)**

6. Many graduate jobs are graduate jobs not because they require the academic rigour of a degree, but because they require the kind of social capital it takes three years at an elite institution to accrue. Simply replacing a degree with an apprenticeship might provide similar networking opportunities and similar – even superior – professional training, but this difference in status will likely still apply. Here the history of spy recruitment can point the way, too. The day-to-day reality of MI6 probably involves as much tedium and petty stationery-based conflict as any other job, but Bond films and John le Carré* novels have convinced us of its glamour. Might apprenticeships in less glamorous-sounding industries benefit from a similar image overhaul?

j) In your own words, explain the main point the writer is making in paragraph 7. (Do not refer to the specific examples given.) **(2 marks)**

7. A successful apprenticeship scheme has the potential to promote social equality, increase individual job satisfaction and improve professional standards. But if it is to fulfil this potential, even targeting traditional graduate professions won't be enough. The apprenticeship route must be made attractive, both to teenagers with no other options and to those who in previous generations would follow their parents into a university education regardless of their personal academic aptitude.

k) How does the example given in paragraph 8 illustrate the main point from the previous paragraph? **(2 marks)**

8. In other words, school-leaver spies are a good thing, but we are going to need more posh plumbers, too.

* John Le Carré: Writer of spy novels set in the Cold War era.
(*Source:* Ellen E. Jones, *The Gulf Today*)

Extra questions

1. In the first four paragraphs, the writer explores the idea of apprentice spies. How does the **tone** of this section contrast with her tone in the second half of the article? Use examples to illustrate your answer. **(4 marks)**
2. Using your own words as far as possible, sum up in bullet-point form the arguments made by the writer in favour of apprenticeships. You should make at least four bullet points. **(4 marks)**

THE FORMAT OF THE PAPER

The Higher English Reading for Understanding, Analysis and Evaluation paper is worth 30 marks and you are given one hour and thirty minutes to complete it in the exam. There will be two passages to read. The first is followed by detailed close reading questions on content and style, while the second has only one question, which asks you to compare the two passages.

Look again at what the terms 'understanding', 'analysis' and 'evaluation' mean.

Understanding

This refers to the content or ideas of the passage: to **what** the writer is saying. Questions of this type are likely to begin with the word **identify** or **explain**.

For example:

> From the first paragraph, **identify** two feelings the writer had as she watched the tree in her garden being cut back.   **(2 marks)**

You should answer this question in your own words. In most cases, there will be two or more points to identify, and there is likely to be one mark awarded per point. 'Lifted' answers – i.e. words copied straight out of the passage – will gain no marks.

Analysis

This refers to the style or techniques used in the passage; to **how** the writer is conveying his meaning. Questions of this type are likely to begin with the word **analyse**.

For example:

> **Analyse** how the writer's use of language in lines ... emphasises the importance of trees   **(4 marks)**

There may also be some guidance as to which language features you should discuss.

For example:

> You should refer in your answer to such features as sentence structure, word choice, imagery, tone...

In answering questions of this type, you are expected to do the following:

- Identify features of language.
- Discuss their relationship with the ideas of the passage as a whole.

Marks will depend on the quality of the answer. Two marks may be awarded for a detailed and insightful comment on a single language feature; one mark would be given for a more basic explanation. If you simply identify a language feature and do not analyse its effect, however, you will not be awarded any marks.

Evaluation

'To evaluate' means to assess the value of and to make a judgement.

For example:

> **Evaluate** the effectiveness of the final paragraph as a conclusion to the passage as a whole. **(2 marks)**

Here, you could refer to the ideas or the style of the passage, or to both.

A word often used in analysis and evaluation questions is 'effective'. An answer like 'The writer's conclusion is very effective' is meaningless: you must go on to say that 'It is effective *because…*'

In general, a feature of a passage will be effective if it adds to the reader's understanding and appreciation of the writer's message. If your answer shows *how* the feature helps you to appreciate what the writer is saying, you are likely to score a high mark.

PRACTICE PAPER 1

A Healthy Diet

The following two passages consider the connection between diet and health.

Passage 1

In the first passage Tom Chivers, writing in the Daily Telegraph, *discusses a recent research study into the effects of animal protein on health.*

Read the passage below and attempt the questions which follow.

You'd be forgiven for looking warily at your bacon sandwich this morning, if you've seen headlines suggesting that a diet high in animal proteins is nearly as dangerous as smoking. Cheese and meat cause cancer! That carbonara is a time-bomb ticking in your stomach! Quick, go vegetarian!

5   The news is based on a study in the journal *Cell Metabolism*, which found that people who got more than a fifth of their daily calories from animal protein were 74 per cent more likely to have died during the study than people who ate less animal protein. We're bombarded with food messages like this, which often seem to change from day to day. Dame Sally Davies, the Chief Medical Officer, has warned about the 'addictive' potential of sugar; the World Health
10 Organization said yesterday that recommended sugar allowances were too high; an editorial in the journal *Open Heart*, also published yesterday, suggested that the risk of saturated fats was overblown.

Every Christmas, suddenly, red wine and chocolate become good for us. Last year headlines screamed that eating three sausages a day raises our risk of dying of heart disease by
15 three-quarters. It's hard to know what to make of it all, the what's-curing-me-and-killing-me-today merry-go-round.

Can eating burgers really be as bad for you as smoking? Before answering that, it's worth looking at how we know how bad for you smoking is.

In the late forties, a man called Richard Doll was given the task of finding out what was
20 behind the dramatic increase in lung cancer deaths. Originally, he and his colleagues thought it was probably the new practice of coating roads with Tarmac. But upon interviewing 649 men with lung cancer in 20 London hospitals, he found one remarkable fact: all but two of them were smokers (he also interviewed a smaller group of women, in which the divide was less dramatic but still very large). He promptly quit smoking. His research had found a simple
25 fact: smoking causes lung cancer, and in fact is the cause of almost all lung cancers.

This caused great excitement. Researchers wondered if other cancers, or other diseases, could be linked as straightforwardly to lifestyle factors. The science of epidemiology – of the causes of disease in populations – had its greatest success since Dr John Snow showed that unclean water caused London's cholera outbreaks in the nineteenth century.

30 But smoking was a low-hanging fruit. There aren't very many straightforwardly poisonous things that lots of humans imbibe in large amounts and lots of humans don't touch at all. Working out whether a particular food is good for you, for instance, is fantastically tricky:

you can't prescribe someone a course of celery for 20 years, and compare how well they do in relation to someone on a celery placebo. You have to rely on people reporting what
35 they eat, which they do only unreliably. And unless you have very large samples, it's hard to tease out causes from mere correlations: how can we know whether celery makes you live longer, or whether people who eat celery tend to live healthier lives generally?

What's more, the body is very complex, so plausible hypotheses about what will do you good and do you harm often turn out to be false. This is why you should ignore anyone who
40 tells you that you ought to eat pomegranate or chia seeds because they're good for your liver, or whatever. They have no idea what they're talking about.

Epidemiologists have, however, been able to tease out broader-brush factors. Red meat, salt, sugar, fat and alcohol are all bad for you in large amounts; eating plenty of fruit and veg is good for you. But exactly how good and how bad, and how much of each you should have,
45 is all very much in dispute. The *Cell Metabolism* study found a huge increase in cancer risk from animal-protein-rich diets, but most earlier research on related topics had found a far less dramatic impact, of between 10 and 15 per cent.

And that's the key. None of these studies is the final truth; science is incremental, it learns by degrees, and epidemiology doubly so. Meat, in large quantities, is probably a bit more
50 dangerous than we previously thought, but to say that it is suddenly as dangerous as smoking is to run far ahead of the evidence. And, of course, there are other differences: it's very difficult to include cigarettes as part of a balanced diet, for instance. Richard Doll's discovery paved the way for a remarkable age of public health research, which has led to us knowing far more about what helps us live longer and what kills us than we did
55 half a century ago. But the picture is usually cloudier than university PR departments like to admit. After decades of study, the best, most well-supported advice is still what your mother told you: eat your greens and get plenty of exercise.

(*Source:* Tom Chivers, *Daily Telegraph*)

Questions

1. Re-read lines 1–4.
   a) Explain why, according to the writer, a bacon sandwich might cause its consumer sudden anxiety. **(2 marks)**
   b) Analyse how the writer's use of language in these lines conveys his meaning effectively. You should refer in your answer to such features as sentence structure, word choice, imagery, tone… **(4 marks)**
2. Re-read lines 5–16.
   By referring to at least two examples, analyse how the writer's use of imagery in this section emphasises the alarmist nature of reports on diet. **(4 marks)**
3. Explain the purpose of lines 17–18 in the presentation of the writer's argument, and analyse how the sentence structure assists in this purpose. **(3 marks)**
4. From lines 19–29 identify two successful outcomes from research connecting health with lifestyle factors. **(2 marks)**
5. Re-read lines 30–47.
   a) Identify any four reasons given in these lines to account for the difficulty of doing satisfactory research into the effects of diet on health. You should use your own words as far as possible. **(4 marks)**
   b) By referring to at least two features of language in lines 30–47, analyse how the writer conveys his meaning effectively. You should refer in your answer to such features as sentence structure, word choice, imagery, contrast, tone… **(4 marks)**
6. Evaluate the final paragraph's effectiveness as a conclusion to the passage as a whole. **(2 marks)**

Total: 25 marks

Passage 2

In the second passage below, from the Guardian, *David Adam discusses the so-called 'caveman diet'.*

Read the passage and attempt the question which follows. While reading, you may wish to make notes on the main ideas and/or highlight key points in the passage.

Would eating a Stone Age diet make us healthier? If only things were that simple. Supporters of the so called Stone Age diet argue that farming practices introduced about 10,000 years ago are ultimately harmful to human health, and that if our hunter-gatherer ancestors evolved without eating dairy products or cereals then we shouldn't eat them
5 either. Instead, they say, we should eat only plenty of lean meat and fish, with fruit and raw vegetables on the side.

The idea, also called the caveman, hunter-gatherer or paleolithic diet, has been around for decades and is regularly recycled – as it was in various newspapers earlier this week after the regime was discussed at a meeting of the British Society for Allergy, Environmental and
10 Nutritional Medicine.

According to Loren Cordain, a nutritionist at Colorado State University who presented the idea to the meeting and published a book about it last year called *The Paleo Diet*, those following the meat-dominated menu 'lose weight and get healthy by eating the food you were designed to eat'. He says there is increasing evidence that a paleolithic diet can prevent
15 and treat many common Western diseases. Studies of islanders in Papua New Guinea who still live a hunter-gatherer lifestyle show they rarely suffer heart disease, for instance.

But other nutritionists argue that, as with the closely related Atkins Diet, cutting out whole food groups such as cereals is just not a good idea.

'I would recommend anybody to eat lean meat and raw vegetables,' says Toni Steer of the
20 MRC human nutrition research unit at Cambridge. 'But what you're asking people to do is cut out a food group that we have a lot of evidence to show is good for your health.'

Archaeologists say it's not even clear exactly how much of the various foods people actually ate during the Stone Age (broadly defined as from two-and-a-half million years ago until 10,000 years ago).

25 'There was no one Stone Age diet; diets of the past varied greatly,' says John Gowlett, an archaeologist at Liverpool University who also attended the conference. People in Africa probably ate less meat than many people think, he says, while those in the northern, icy regions were forced to eat only whatever animals they could catch.

'I'm not convinced that we know what Stone Age man ate,' agrees Andrew Millard, who
30 researches ancient health and diet at Durham University. 'The evidence we have is heavily biased towards the meat component of the diet. We get bones from animals they have eaten but we don't get the remains of any vegetables they have eaten because they decay.'

Millard adds that there is good evidence that later Stone Age cultures in the Near East regularly collected and ate wild cereals and it's possible the practice was more widespread.

(*Source:* David Adam, *Guardian* (adapted))

Question

7. Both writers report on research into the effects of diet on health. David Adam's passage was written ten years earlier than Tom Chivers'. Identify key similarities and differences in their reports. In your answer, you should refer in detail to both passages.
   You may answer this question in continuous prose or in a series of developed bullet points. **(5 marks)**

PRACTICE PAPER 2

Dogs

The following two passages focus on different attitudes towards dogs.

Passage 1

In the first passage Sarah Vine, writing in the Daily Mail, *describes her experience of owning a bichon frise puppy.*

Read the passage below and attempt the questions which follow.

The date was late January, cold and dark. Dirty snow on the ground, and nothing but credit card bills, detox shakes and tax returns: the gloomiest, most depressing time of year. Perhaps that was what made me do it; that, and the fact that I'm a sucker for a sob story. He was an unwanted Christmas present, they said. A small, male, bichon frise puppy, ten
5 weeks old. Eyes like chocolate buttons, fur as soft as pussy willow, all wobbly and scared. Also, as I later found out, teeming with fleas and as malodorous as a goat. It was love at first sight.

It was also sheer madness. Aside from the fact that we already had one perfectly excellent dog, a Jack Russell/whippet cross called Mars (now sadly deceased), I have two children
10 and a full-time job. There is not enough room in our house to swing a cat, let alone accommodate a rampaging puppy. But then, dogs are like children: if you think too hard about it, you would never have any at all.

All puppies are, by definition, cute. But a bichon puppy takes the concept to a whole other level. Bichons are the kings of cute, the sultans of soppy, the Olympic champions
15 of adorability. Walk down the street with a bichon, and even traffic wardens are nice to you. It's not just that bichons look adorable; it's also that they *are* adorable. They have the sweetest and sunniest of dispositions, the kindest and most patient of personalities. There is not the first aggressive thought in the space between those fluffy ears of theirs. I have never once heard ours growl, even when dressed in a tutu and fairy wings, or being
20 wheeled around the house in a doll's pram.

Owning a bichon is basically like having a very jolly, very affectionate and slightly greedy toddler around the place. Like most toddlers, ours – Snowy – can't really be left alone. Woe betide us if we try to go out, even for the shortest of times. The look on his face as we depart for the school run is such a skilful combination of anguish and resentment, I sometimes wonder
25 whether he might not be the reincarnation of some great actor. I picture Marlon Brando … trapped in the body of an overgrown teddy bear. In the early days his separation anxiety was so extreme we had to have him with us at all times. I actually became one of those mad women who keep a dog in their handbag, since as well as being clingy he was also incredibly lazy. We would take him for walks, and he would simply lie down and refuse to get up again. At
30 one point I even contemplated getting him a doggy pram, until my husband explained that he would actually have to leave if I did. There was also an issue with cleanliness.

→

→

Mars was one of those wonderful short-haired, self-cleaning dogs. Snowy, on the other hand, makes Lady Gaga look low-maintenance. He needs twice weekly baths and regular trims, and because bichons don't shed their hair (which also makes them suitable for

35 people who are allergic to dogs), he requires regular brushing to avoid matting. Despite my best efforts, he still looks like a dirty sheepskin rug most days (hence his nickname Sheepy). But he loves his baths so much that he has been known to jump in with the children – to their great delight – whereupon he immediately shrinks to half his size and you realise what a terrible weed he is beneath all that white fluff.

40 One of the trickiest things about bichons is their dim grasp of the concept of personal space. Having had one very obedient dog that slept downstairs in his designated bed and only came up in the morning to respectfully request that I open the back door, it took me some time before I realised that this was simply not an arrangement Snowy's bichon brain could compute. Some progress has now been made, in that he now no longer sleeps on my actual head or underneath

45 my pillow, and he has given up trying to perch on my shoulder like a parrot when I'm driving the car. But if I shut the bedroom door even for a minute, he throws himself at it with the violence and desperation of someone trapped in the boot of a car that is slowly sinking.

Elsewhere, he can be a terrible diva. Can I get him to use the dog-flap, installed at vast expense? Can I hell. My daughter and I spent an entire week trying to coax him in and

50 out through the damn thing with bits of roast chicken, to no avail. She even tried to demonstrate, by putting her head through it herself, whereupon she got stuck and had to be eased back out with olive oil behind the ears. He simply carried on pawing at the woodwork.

Speaking of expense, owning a bichon is not a cost-neutral exercise. They steal constantly: toothbrushes, shoes, tights, toys, post. You name it, if Snowy can carry it, he'll pinch it – and

55 then chew it to death. The shoes are a bit of an issue: a pup psychologist might say he's trying to stop us from going out by systematically devouring all the footwear in the house. His favourite (and the most financially disastrous) are my husband's work shoes and the children's school ones; he also destroyed my favourite boots, bought on holiday in Italy a few years ago, and shredded my trendy black and yellow wedges.

60 Expensive footwear aside, the bichon's other obsession is food. He will break into the bin, raid the vegetable patch and lick the pavement in search of the tiniest, most rancid of morsels. He once broke into a bag of cheese that a guest had brought to dinner; and I still haven't quite forgiven him for the time he ate an entire sushi takeaway, chopsticks included. Last week, in the time it took me to unload the shopping into the fridge, he

65 managed to get his nose into a large bag of guinea pig feed, only to spend the next few hours throwing up all over the house.

The thing is, though, we love him. Whenever he has one of his 'bichon blitzes' (a characteristic of the breed, in which they charge around like loons until collapsing exhausted), we all join in. It's very silly, of course, and wholly undignified, but somehow

70 chasing a mad white furball around the park makes me happy in ways I had never imagined possible. But that's bichons for you: incorrigible but thoroughly irresistible.

(*Source:* Sarah Vine, *Daily Mail*)

Questions

1. Read again lines 1–4, to '…they said.'
   a) Using your own words, identify two reasons why the writer was inclined to take the dog. **(2 marks)**
   b) Analyse how the writer's use of language in lines 4–7 conveys her feelings for the dog. You should refer in your answer to such features as sentence structure, word choice, imagery, contrast, tone… **(4 marks)**
2. Read again lines 8–12.
   In your own words, suggest two reasons the writer had not to take the puppy. **(2 marks)**
3. By referring to at least two features of language in lines 13–20, analyse how the writer conveys the characteristics of a bichon frise. You should refer in your answer to such features as sentence structure, word choice, imagery, tone… **(4 marks)**
4. Read again lines 21–39.
   By referring to at least two features of language in this section, analyse how the writer conveys the problems she faces with her dog in a humorous way. You should refer in your answer to such features as sentence structure, word choice, imagery, tone… **(4 marks)**
5. Re-read lines 40–66.
   a) Identify any three behaviour problems the writer had to face with her dog. You should use your own words as far as possible. **(3 marks)**
   b) By referring to at least two examples, analyse how the writer's use of sentence structure is effective in conveying these behaviour problems. **(4 marks)**
6. Evaluate the final paragraph's effectiveness as a conclusion to the passage as a whole. **(2 marks)**

Total: 25 marks

Passage 2

In the second passage below, writer Grant Feller gives his own views on dogs in an online blog.

Read the passage and attempt the question that follows. While reading, you may wish to make notes on the main ideas and/or highlight key points in the passage.

I have a terrible confession to make. One that will alienate friends, enrage neighbours and no doubt instigate a cacophony of online abuse.

I hate dogs. I mean I don't just hate them, in a 'shoo, leave me alone' way. I really genuinely hate them. Not their owners – not all of them anyway – just their smelly, waste-producing,
5 noisy, over-enthusiastic, straining-at-the-chains, handbag-sized, fluffy, doe-eyed, saliva-sharing, wet-nosed pets.

It's not just the dogs that upset me, though. It's the marginalisation of dog-haters in society, the instant labelling of us as cold-hearted, deeply troubled, anger-fuelled, emotionally stunted. Admittedly, I might be all of those actually, but my four-pawed prejudice doesn't
10 automatically mean I am.

In Cornwall last year – out of season, October – I was walking with my young son on a windswept beach with the tide out, picking up shells (surely one of the best ever father–child bonding exercises), when out of the corner of my eye I spied a big thing hurtling towards us. Within seconds it had jumped up on its hind legs, its other two limbs resting on
15 my son's chest until he fell over, his screams drowned out by the dog's barks.

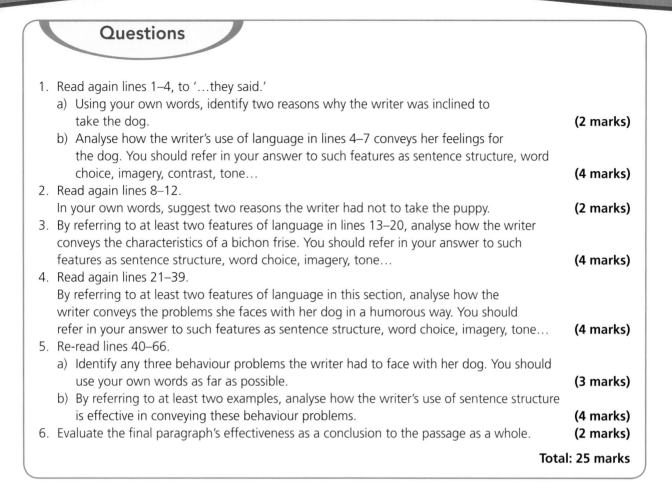

➡

'Oh, he just wants to play,' said the laughing owner. 'He just loves children.' I stood open-mouthed, waiting for the apology that didn't come. 'I love children too,' I replied, 'and if I ran towards one and knocked one to the ground by jumping on top with my tongue hanging out and shouting loudly, would you like it?'

20 And then last week I had an early evening barbecue for friends, one of whom turned up with their new coochie-poochie-woochie in their arms, breezed happily past me and proceeded to let their 'best friend' run around my postage stamp garden and feed off scraps of the unbelievably expensive designer sausages I had expertly cooked for human consumption. (I remember happily sitting in the car with a cola, some crisps and the
25 window slightly open when my dad took me somewhere I wasn't invited.)

She didn't even ask permission. That's because we've reached the stage where dog owning is the norm and everyone who doesn't own one is considered weird.

What's wrong with them barking at 11:30 p.m. or before Radio 4's *Today* programme comes on air – they're just expressing themselves! They have become extensions of our
30 human selves in a way that couldn't have been imagined in previous centuries. And as such they've taken on, according to their deluded owners anyway, human characteristics. Intelligence, empathy, personality, sense of humour. Perhaps owners see in their animals something they lack.

(*Source:* Grant Feller, *Huffington Post* (adapted))

Question

7. Both writers express their feelings towards dogs. Identify key areas where their attitudes differ. In your answer, you should refer in detail to both passages.
   You may answer this question in continuous prose or in a series of developed bullet points.   **(5 marks)**

PRACTICE PAPER 3

Old Age

The following two passages focus on attitudes to old age.

Passage 1

In the first passage, A.A. Gill, writing in The Sunday Times Magazine, *considers how society treats old people.*

Read the passage below and attempt the questions that follow.

I want you to do something for me. Think of it as a game, a quiz, a trick. Go and find an old person – one who's not related to you or a neighbour. Just a random, strange old person, a lurking crusty. Look at this old person, stare at them, get really close. Don't be frightened – they won't hurt you. They're not contagious; they're more frightened of you than you are of

5 them. Right, here's the game bit. Can you tell me how old they actually are? Look carefully at that face, at the wrinkles, the sunken cheeks, the frail, eroded jaw. Count the archipelagos of age spots, examine the wind-coloured hair patted into the habit of a lifetime. Look into the fretted, damp eyes, their lids sagging like ragged bedroom curtains, and add up the years. Pick a number, like guessing the weight of a cake or the height of a steeple. You'll see

10 it's much more difficult than it looks.

You can discern the years between 16 and 20. You know a 21-year-old from a 28-year-old, but I bet you can't mark a decade between 60 and 90. You can't read the gradations and patinas. Not that old people hide them; you can't tell because you don't look. And you don't look because you don't care. Really, who cares how old the old are? Old is a destination.

15 There is nothing after old, just nothing. Old is not a number; it's not a date. It's simply the absence of youth, the absence of attraction, interest, new friends, society. The absence of conviviality, warmth, choice, or surprise, or life.

We have a problem with old age, a huge problem. If we arbitrarily cut the birthday cake at 65, then that makes the old 17.6 per cent of the population, which will rise to 22 per cent by

20 2031. The old use up more than 40 per cent of the national health budget. But the old aren't the problem – it's the rest of us. It's you and I who have the problem. It's our collective refusal to look at the old, to be in a room with them, to ask them into our lives. The great terror of our age is age. We would rather consign the old to a netherworld, a waiting room where they are out of mind, and out of sight. The fear is plainly not of the old: it is that we

25 will become them. The old are the zombies at the end of our own home horror movies.

We are one of the very few cultures in all the world, down all the ages, that don't treat age as an achievement in and of itself. There are no old people's homes in Africa, because the old live with their families and in their communities. They earn honorific titles – white hair and a stick are owed respect. There is a polite assumption of wisdom in experience. But

30 we are terrified of the loss of youth. We kick against the clock, like infants trying to put off bedtime. We dress younger than we are, stretch, freeze and stitch our sagging bodies to fool those younger than ourselves, as if a cocktail of lentils, beetroot juice, positive thinking and hip-hop talk will make us 30 for ever.

→

→

35 Ageing is so frightening in part because we treat the old so badly, and we treat them badly because we're so frightened of them. We ignore them and consign them to horrible solitude because we can't face the truth that someday someone will banish us. Most people in this country die weepingly lonely – cold, starved, and left in no doubt that they have overstayed their welcome. This is the greatest shame and horror of our society and our age.

40 The cure for this youth-tormented terror is blindingly simple. Reclaim the old. Include them in our lives. The antibiotic for loneliness is company. I wouldn't patronise the aged by claiming that everything they say is wise or steeped in the rare tincture of experience. They talk as much repetitive nonsense as the rest of us. But we never listen to them; we're deaf to the old. We assume they have nothing to tell us, nothing but loopy non-sequiturs and circular complaints.

45 You know, you really should spend an hour listening to someone who's lived twice as long as you, not as social philanthropy or goodness, but for your own sake, for the sake of your self-worth, to calm your speechless fears about ageing, and because you'll hear something funny and clever, touching and probably astonishing. Most old people are more interesting than most young people, simply because they're older. Experience may not bring wisdom, but it does make for some cracking stories. Every old person you ignore has lived through

50 times and done things, seen stuff that you never will, and it's worth hearing about.

There is a towering, pitiful irony that one of the most popular uses of the net is unravelling genealogy. We will spend hours picking through turgid ledgers and ancient lists to discover whom we are, but can't bring ourselves to listen to the first-hand account of where we come from and what it was like.

55 We should, at the very least, ensure that nobody, none of our kin, compatriots, kith or countrymen, ever sits alone wishing for their own death because they know of nobody who wishes them to live. We will abate our own fears of ageing by ensuring that someone else isn't fearful and lonely. You get back what you give.

(*Source:* A. A. Gill, *The Sunday Times Magazine*)

Questions

1. Re-read paragraph 1 (lines 1–10).
   a) From lines 1–5, explain what is involved in the 'game' the writer invites the reader to play. **(2 marks)**
   b) Analyse how the writer's use of language in lines 5–10 emphasises society's negative view of old people. You should refer in your answer to such features as sentence structure, word choice, imagery, tone… **(4 marks)**
2. Re-read paragraph 2 (lines 11–17).
   Identify what the author believes the 'game' will demonstrate. **(2 marks)**
3. Re-read paragraph 3 (lines 18–25).
   By referring to at least **two** features of language, analyse how the writer conveys people's fear of old age. **(4 marks)**
4. Re-read paragraph 4 (lines 26–33).
   Identify the differences between attitudes to age in Western countries and in other parts of the world such as Africa. **(4 marks)**

→

Questions

5. Re-read paragraph 5 (lines 34–38).
    a) Identify what the writer considers to be the 'greatest shame and horror of our society and
        our age'.   **(2 marks)**
    b) Analyse how his word choice conveys the strength of his feelings about this.   **(3 marks)**
6. Evaluate the final paragraph's effectiveness as a conclusion to the passage as a whole.   **(4 marks)**

                                                                                    Total: 25 marks

Passage 2

In the second passage, Lonnette Harrell argues that 'attitude is everything'.

Read the passage and attempt the question which follows. While reading, you may wish
to make notes on the main ideas and/or highlight key points in the passage.

In the American culture, which is so youth-oriented, the elderly have become invisible, and
are greatly devalued by society. Yet many seniors still find great joy in living. According to
a recent study, attitude is the most important factor. Five hundred Americans between the
ages of 60 and 98 were studied. They all lived independently, and had experienced many

5 illnesses including cancer, heart disease, diabetes and mental health concerns. They were
asked to rate themselves on successful ageing, on a scale from 1 to 10, with 10 being the
best. Surprisingly enough, in spite of their health problems, the average rating was 8.4. Dilip
Jeste, lead researcher of the University of California at San Diego, stated, 'These findings
suggest that physical health is not the best indicator of successful ageing – attitude is.'

10 Old age can be a time to reinvent yourself, to find a different focus or career, to try new
things, and to realise past dreams. In fact, many actors, scientists, politicians, statesmen,
teachers, writers, and Nobel Peace Prize winners have been most productive in their senior
years. Mother Teresa was almost 70 when she received her Nobel Peace Prize. Benjamin
Franklin was 70 when he helped edit the Declaration of Independence.

15 The senior years provide a wonderful opportunity to be a mentor – to impart the knowledge
that life has given you. Youthful thinking can be an inspiration to the old, and the wisdom
of age can bring great enlightenment to the young.

Moreover, it is important to develop close relationships. Often in the retirement years,
people have lost many friendships from their workplace and feel isolated. Some

20 psychologists believe that when there are few social connections, greater depression
occurs. Taking care of a grandchild, or doing volunteer work, may be life-enhancing during
the retirement years, giving the person a feeling of achievement and productivity.

A spiritual connection is also helpful. According to research in Europe and North America,
religiously active people are happier than those who are not religiously involved. In

25 study after study, elderly people report being happier when they are active in a church
or religious setting, and widows who worship regularly also report more joy in their lives.
Again, there is a vital network of social support in the spiritual community, as well as
purpose in reaching out to others.

Laura Carstensen, director of the Stanford Center of Longevity, has found that people

30 generally get happier as they age. She attributes the greater happiness to a desire to make

→

the most of the time left. She stated, 'When people perceive time is limited, they focus more on wellbeing.' Research by Gene Cohen, a psychiatrist, gerontologist, and director of George Washington University's Center on Ageing, Health and Humanities, supports this theory. He found that brain function changes as a person ages. Imaging studies have shown
35   that older people's brains react less intensely, and for less time, to negative emotions. This contributes to increased morale in old age. Older people become more experienced in handling problems and challenges, and they may have also lowered their expectations, thereby making it easier to experience happiness.

To a great degree, true happiness comes from within. Many elderly people seem to have
40   a radiance reflected from a life well-lived. It has been said that 'the happy person sees rainbows everywhere.' The unhappy person only sees rain. Outlook is so vital to satisfaction in life. Nothing external can give you the peace and calmness that comes from inner joy. So if you desire to age gracefully, and happily, *attitude* is everything.

(*Source:* Lonnette Harrell, voices.yahoo.com)

Question

7. Both writers discuss their views on old age and the treatment of the elderly. Identify key areas where they express different opinions. In your answer, you should refer in detail to both passages.
You may answer this question in continuous prose or in a series of developed bullet points. **(5 marks)**

PRACTICE PAPER 4

Cycling

The following two passages focus on attitudes to cycling.

Passage 1

In the first passage, from The Herald *newspaper, Alan Taylor argues that it is time 'to make cyclists pay their own way'.*

Read the passage below and attempt the questions that follow.

Nirvana for cyclists is The Netherlands. It is where they all are desperate to go before they wear out their saddles. It is their promised land, their Mecca where cycling is taken more seriously than any religion, where bikes are treated with proper reverence.

In The Netherlands there are more bikes than people as there were once more sheep than
5   people in Scotland. You will not be surprised to learn, therefore, that almost everyone cycles daily. Indeed, children often cycle several miles back and forth to school and every shop is obliged to provide cycle racks at its door.

Such popularity breeds political clout. No one who aspires to power dare ignore the cycling lobby. Thus all new roads have cycle lanes, which are separated from cars by a raised verge.
10 For those who wish to cycle without the din of traffic in their ears the number of dedicated cycle paths is legion.

Best of all, however, is the fact that The Netherlands is flat. There, only fusspots or the fatally unfit bother to buy bikes with eighteen gears. Moreover, most bikes weigh a ton. With no hills to negotiate, it is unnecessary to invest in super-light machines that cost
15 more than replacement body parts.

Short of steamrollering the Cairngorms and other bumpy parts of Scotland there is no way we can compete with what used to be called the Low Countries. Cyclists here know that they are in a never-ending battle with geography and climate. If the hills don't do you in the wind probably will.

20 Hence the look of strained stoicism on most cyclists' faces. To be a cyclist in Scotland is not for the faint-hearted. Rather it is for those of a fundamentalist mind, for those who can see in their mind's eye the promised land but who, in order to reach it, must cross an eight-lane motorway thundering with juggernauts.

Take, if you will, Graeme Obree, a world champion cyclist who famously made his favourite
25 bike, Old Faithful, out of bits of dead washing machine. Obree, like so many members of the cycling cult, would love Scotland to be like The Netherlands or, at a push, Germany.

At the weekend, with 14,000 other two-wheeled fanatics, he rode from Saltcoats to Glasgow as part of a cycling pilgrimage. At its end he could not resist having a wee moan, saying that cyclists need more protection from the cars that invade their lanes and force them
30 into the mainstream of traffic whereupon accidents occur. 'Some roads,' said Obree, 'are just not user-friendly like they are in Europe.'

→

→

No doubt his fellow cyclists cheered when they heard these words. As with all minorities they seem to nurse a permanent sense of grievance. On top of which they exude righteousness. Not only are they keeping themselves fit, they chirrup, they are saving the
35   planet while doing so.

Excuse me if I choose to throw a spanner or two into their spokes. In my experience, that of a bus-using pedestrian, cyclists are often no better or worse than motorists. If they've actually read the Highway Code many of them pay it scant heed.

Unlike motorists, cyclists hunt in packs. Even when there are lanes for which they've
40   campaigned, they wilfully ignore them. On twisting country roads, they ride two or more abreast, as if to goad motorists who can either crash into them or tag on to the back of the peloton and wait interminably for a clear stretch of road to overtake.

As the number of cyclists continues to increase and the cries for better provision grow ever more hysterical it is time they were made to pay their way. First, I suggest each bike should
45   have number plates, which would allow miscreants to be identified and informed upon.

Second, the introduction of an annual licence fee – £20 seems reasonable – such as that payable by TV owners, would allow cyclists to argue for an improvement of their lot from the moral high ground. Which, needless to say, can only be reached in the lowest of low gears.

(*Source:* Alan Taylor, *The Herald*)

Questions

1. Re-read lines 1–3.
    Analyse how the writer's use of imagery helps the reader to understand the attitude
    taken in The Netherlands towards cycling.   **(3 marks)**
2. Re-read lines 4–15.
    Identify any **four** aspects of cycling in The Netherlands that differ from Scotland. **(4 marks)**
3. Re-read lines 16–23.
    By referring to at least **two** features of language, analyse how the writer conveys the
    difficulties of being a cyclist in Scotland.
    You should refer to such features as sentence structure, word choice, imagery…   **(3 marks)**
4. Re-read lines 27–36.
    a) Explain the writer's personal opinion of cycling enthusiasts.   **(2 marks)**
    b) By referring to at least **two** examples, show how his use of word choice and/or
        imagery helps to convey this opinion.   **(4 marks)**
5. Re-read lines 39–42.
    Identify **three** criticisms the writer makes of the behaviour of cyclists on the roads. **(3 marks)**
6. Re-read lines 43–49.
    The writer suggests two specific measures that should be taken to regulate cyclists.
    Identify these measures and explain what he considers their advantages to be.   **(4 marks)**
7. Evaluate the final paragraph's effectiveness as a conclusion to the passage as a whole. **(2 marks)**

Total: 25 marks

Passage 2

In the second passage, also from The Herald, *Susan Swarbrick writes in praise of cycling.*

Read the passage and attempt the question which follows. While reading, you may wish to make notes on the main ideas and/or highlight key points in the passage.

There have been murmurings among my nearest and dearest that I have a habit. A lone word lingers perpetually on my tongue: cycling.

Last Sunday I joined 7285 other riders to traverse the winding back roads from Glasgow to Edinburgh on the Pedal for Scotland 47-mile challenge. We were buffeted by crosswinds
5 and drenched with icy rain, but I loved every second. Not even the L'Alpe de Falkirk – aka the beast of a hill outside Avonbridge – could break me.

As addictions go, admittedly it is spiralling. When not conversing with fellow cycling geeks on Twitter, I'm flicking through specialist magazines or gazing in awe at photographs of my dream road bike.

10 During this summer's Tour de France I recorded and watched every stage. Not the highlights, the whole shebang. Some evenings my viewing would stretch upwards of four hours. I often didn't get to bed until after 1 a.m., spending the whole three weeks bleary-eyed yet unwavering in my devotion. There is a whimsical romanticism to cycling that I have yet to find in other sports. Few sights are more enthralling than a panning aerial shot
15 of a professional peloton in full flight across open countryside.

The mesmerising spectacle of a rainbow of jerseys packed tightly together on a steep incline always puts me in mind of salmon battling their way upstream, sublime and raw in its beauty.

Gladiatorial in construct yet entrancingly elegant, cycling is a world where unwritten
20 gentleman's rules and old-fashioned etiquette govern the peloton as much as team orders.

There are brotherly allegiances and bitter rivalries. They crash, break bones, get back in the saddle again. Winning comes not just from skill and mastery but from the ability to suffer longest.

Cycling equates to passion, escapism and camaraderie. And therein lies the magic.

(*Source:* Susan Swarbrick, *The Herald*)

Question

8. Both writers express their views on cyclists. Identify the areas where they agree and the areas where they disagree. In your answer, you should refer in detail to both passages.
   You may answer this question in continuous prose or in a series of developed bullet points. **(5 marks)**

GRAMMAR AND SYNTAX

As was explained in Part One (Reading Skills), questions on sentence structure require you to demonstrate your understanding of how language is put together – how paragraphs and sentences are assembled.

The technical terms for this are grammar and syntax. **Syntax** is the arrangement of words and phrases in a sentence, and **grammar** is the body of rules according to which such arrangements are made.

Writers aim to achieve certain effects through syntax, and you will be expected to recognise, identify and explain these techniques. Obviously, the more you know about grammar and syntax, the better able you will be to appreciate their particular application within writers' work. The following section will give you a brief summing up of some of the basic principles of grammar and will explain some of the terminology that is used.

SENTENCES, CLAUSES AND PHRASES

A **sentence** is a group of words that contains a verb and makes complete sense. A sentence may be a **statement**, a **question**, an **exclamation** or a **command**:

- 'John is sitting down.'

- 'Is John sitting down?'

- 'John is sitting down!'

- 'Sit down, John.'

A basic knowledge of **sentence analysis** is useful, and can enable you to discuss an author's techniques with more authority. You may be able to note if a part of a sentence seems to be missing, or if a sentence has an unusual formation. For example, if there is no verb, the construction is called a **minor sentence** or said to be in **note form**.

A sentence can be split into various elements. The **subject** is the topic that is being discussed. The **predicate** is what is said about the subject; it contains the verb of the sentence.

Here are three examples of sentences, all of which have the same subject:

Subject	Predicate
The dog	killed the rat.
	gave his master the stick.
	ran across the road.

'Predicate' is not in itself a particularly useful term, but an analysis of different patterns of predicate can be helpful.

The predicate always contains the **verb** of the sentence: 'killed', 'gave' and 'ran' in the examples above.

The first predicate contains the verb 'killed' plus a **direct object**: 'the rat'. This answers the question 'What did the dog kill?'

The second predicate also contains a verb, 'gave', and a **direct object**, 'the stick', which answers the question 'What did the dog give?' It also contains an **indirect object**, 'his master'. This answers the question 'To whom?'

Verbs that make sense when followed with a direct object, as in these two examples, are called **transitive** verbs.

Some verbs do not require a direct object to make sense. These are called **intransitive** verbs. The third predicate contains such a verb. The question 'What?' does not make sense after 'The dog ran…' This predicate is completed with an **adverbial phrase**: 'across the road'. Such a phrase will answer the question 'Where?', 'When?' or 'How?' Adverbial phrases can also be used in sentences with transitive verbs.

For practice

Questions

Draw a table with five columns, like the one below, and then analyse the following sentences. Remember that you will not have something in each column every time.

a) I told the children a story.
b) The light shone into the room.
c) The aircraft crashed just after take-off.
d) She found the missing money in the tea caddy.

	Subject	Verb	Indirect object	Direct object	Adverbial phrase
a					
b					
c					
d					

WORD ORDER

As discussed on page 25, the normal word order in English is for the **subject** to come first, then the **predicate**:

A stranger stood in the doorway.

Occasionally, however, the subject is delayed and placed after part of the predicate or even after the whole of the predicate, a technique known as **inversion**:

In the doorway stood a stranger.

The use of inversion alters the emphasis. In the above example, the inversion adds suspense as the subject, 'a stranger', is delayed, which throws the spotlight on to it.

For practice

Questions

Consider what effect is obtained in the following examples of inversion. (The conventional word order is given first for purposes of comparison.) Remember that there will only be a slight difference, perhaps of tone or emphasis.

a) His fist smacked down on to the table.
   Down smacked his fist on to the table.
b) The car door opened and the Queen stepped out.
   The car door opened and out stepped the Queen.
c) A beautiful princess lived in a dark and gloomy castle in the middle of a dense forest.
   In the middle of a dense forest, in a dark and gloomy castle, lived a beautiful princess.
d) I have never done that.
   That, I have never done.
e) For Henry Jekyll stood there before my eyes, pale and shaken, and half fainting and groping before him with his hands like a man restored from death!
   For there before my eyes – pale and shaken, and half fainting, and groping before him with his hands like a man restored from death – there stood Henry Jekyll!
(*Source: The Strange Case of Dr Jekyll and Mr Hyde* by R.L. Stevenson)

ACTIVE OR PASSIVE?

Another variation that alters the emphasis in a sentence is the use of the **passive voice**. Usually, the subject performs the action of the verb. But this need not be so.

For example, the sentence

The lion killed the zebra. (Active)

could be rearranged to

The zebra was killed by the lion. (Passive)

In the second sentence 'the zebra' is grammatically the subject, although the action is being done to it. Using the passive voice suggests that the zebra is the main focus of interest.

Notice that the passive often has an **impersonal tone**: this is a construction often used in reports and other situations where **formal** language is desirable. For example,

It was agreed that the meeting should be adjourned.

This is preferred to the more personal, active form: 'We agreed that…' or 'People agreed that…' These structures would sound less formal and official.

For practice

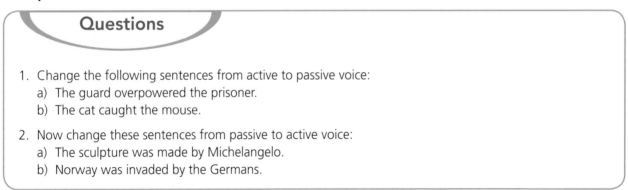

Questions

1. Change the following sentences from active to passive voice:
   a) The guard overpowered the prisoner.
   b) The cat caught the mouse.

2. Now change these sentences from passive to active voice:
   a) The sculpture was made by Michelangelo.
   b) Norway was invaded by the Germans.

CLAUSES, COMPLEX AND SIMPLE SENTENCES

A sentence is composed of one or more 'clauses'. A **clause** is a unit of language containing a subject and a predicate. A **simple sentence** contains one clause only:

The lion killed the zebra.

A **complex sentence** contains more than one clause, but at least one of these clauses must make sense by itself:

Because it needed food for its cubs, the lion killed the zebra.

In this example, the clause 'the lion killed the zebra' could make sense by itself. Such a clause is known as the **principal** or **main** clause. Clauses that cannot stand alone (in this example, 'Because it needed food for its cubs') are called **subordinate** clauses. (A distinction is sometimes made between complex sentences and compound sentences, the latter containing more than one principal clause. In practice this distinction is unlikely to be useful.)

The sentence structure chosen will reflect the subject matter. For example:

- A series of short, simple sentences may build up tension.

- A single simple sentence may make a very dramatic contrast after a series of longer, complex ones.

- A climax may be built up or a surprise created by a series of subordinate clauses followed by a main clause.

- Sometimes a number of simple sentences (each a principal clause) are strung together with 'ands'. This is known as a 'loose' sentence structure. It is used in informal writing or writing that is being made deliberately simple – to suggest boredom, for example.

Subordinate clauses can function as nouns, adjectives or adverbs. Although you will not be asked to identify types of clauses, it can be useful to be able to do so.

- A **noun clause** answers the question 'What?' in response to a main clause. It is usually introduced by 'that' or 'what'. For example,
  He told me *that he would be unable to come.*
  I asked him *what he was doing.*

- An **adjective clause** describes something or someone and is usually introduced by 'who', 'whom', 'which' or (less commonly) 'that'. For example,
  The man *who lives next door* has just won the lottery.
  I lost the book *that I had borrowed from the library.*

- **Adverbial clauses** are of many types and perform various functions. The following four types are among the most common and the most useful to be able to recognise:

- Time (answers the question 'When?'), introduced by 'when', 'before', 'after'. For example,
  When the cat's away, the mice will play.

- Condition (answers the question 'On what condition?'), introduced by 'if' or 'unless'. For example,
  If I see him, I will tell him.

- Reason (answers the question 'Why?'), introduced by 'because', 'as' or 'since'. For example,
  He went home from work *because he felt ill.*

- Concession (answers the question 'In spite of what?'), introduced by 'although'. For example,
  Although he was small, he was strong.

PHRASES

A phrase is a group of words, not including a verb, which forms a unit. For example:

a fat, black cat

with long, fair hair

slowly but surely

in the corner of the room

next Tuesday

Phrases can be used as nouns, adjectives and adverbs. (In the list above, the first example is a noun phrase, the second is an adjectival phrase, and the last three are adverbial phrases of manner, place and time respectively.)

If a sentence contains several phrases of one type, you might comment on this and suggest the effect the writer is aiming at.

PARTS OF SPEECH

Parts of speech is the term given to words according to their function in a piece of writing. The terminology used for this varies, but the traditional method distinguishes eight parts of speech. These are: nouns (common, proper, collective, abstract), verbs, adjectives, adverbs, pronouns, prepositions, conjunctions and articles.

- **Verbs**, perhaps, offer the widest scope for comment. Using many action verbs, for instance, may create a tense, dynamic effect:

  He raced down the hall, wrenched open the door, leapt down the porch steps and flung himself into his car.

- You should be able to recognise **present participles** (which end in -ing). A series of these creates an impression of prolonged or continuing action. Verb **tenses** (past, present and future) may also be worthy of comment. The tense used in most narrative writing is past, but occasionally a **historic present** is used, which adds immediacy or drama to the writing (see passage 5 in the box on page 106).

  We have noted above how a verb may be **active** or **passive**, and it may also be in the form of a **command**, e.g. '*Buy* British!'

- **Adjectives** have three forms: **positive**, **comparative** and **superlative** (as in big – bigger – biggest). Frequent use of comparatives and superlatives is typical of writing that aims to persuade, such as travel brochures or advertisements.

- **Conjunctions** are important. We have already seen (in the section on Link questions on pages 5–6) how conjunctions indicate the linkage of ideas in an argument. The use of 'and' is often particularly significant. It may be omitted where it would normally be expected, which usually has a terse, dramatic effect: 'I came, I saw, I conquered.'

  Alternatively, 'and' may be repeated more frequently than usual. In the following example, the 'ands' emphasise the tediousness of a dinner party:

  The Professor was charming and attentive and told Dolly that he liked her hat, and Mrs Clifford seemed really interested in life at the Coombe Hotel and wanted to hear all about the people who lived there.

  (Source: The Shell Seekers by Rosamunde Pilcher)

It is impossible to cover all the variations that are to be found in the way parts of speech are used, but you should be on the alert for parts of speech used in an unusual way and be prepared to comment. Some writers will have typical mannerisms. One writer habitually uses lists of adjectives without including 'and', frequently in groups of three to create a small climax:

He left the room depressed, dejected, despairing.

SENTENCE STRUCTURE

For practice

Question

Comment on the authors' use of sentence structure in the following pieces of writing and consider their purpose in the techniques they have chosen. You could also comment on any other striking features of style, such as word choice or imagery.

1. (*In the following extract, the character is extremely dissatisfied and bored with life.*)

   The flat crouched around him, watching like a depressed relation, waiting for him to take some action. He drew the curtains and switched on the lamp and things looked marginally better. He took The Times from his coat pocket and tossed it on the table. Pulled off his coat and flung it across a chair. He went into the kitchen and poured a strong whisky and filled the glass with ice from the fridge. He went back to the sitting room and sat down on the sofa and opened the paper.

   (*Source: The Shell Seekers* **by Rosamunde Pilcher**)

2. Ivy is a menace, an invader, the horticultural equivalent of the Mongol hordes who were long supposed to be bashing on the eastern gates of Christendom. Ivy is gloom, an all-conquering bossy-boots, its tendrils harbingers of mankind's decay and the Devil's darkness. It destroys walls, topples trees, smothers individuality. It may even have a whiff of paganism. Ivy in a garden becomes a murderer. Wild flowers stand little chance. They are throttled before they can bloom. Gallant hellebores are crushed. Blameless dwarf narcissi, when threatened by ivy, struggle for life like mice in a cat's claws. The battle only ever ends one way.

   (*Source:* **Quentin Letts,** *Daily Mail*)

3. (*In the following extract two sisters have gone down to a creek for a picnic. When they return home they find that one of the sisters has lost a valuable brooch borrowed from their mother without permission, and so they must carefully retrace their exact steps.*)

   Back we went, searching the bush on which the meadow lark had sung, following our faint trail through the waving grass, refinding the places where the violets were thickest. Down we went on our hands and knees, pushing aside the slim, cool grass with edges that cut the fingers.

   (*Source:* 'Tall Grass' by Maureen Daly)

4. The court was told that Miss Martin had not been at home on the Saturday evening. It was alleged that the accused had entered her house and waited there for her to return. He was said to have threatened her with a knife when she opened the door and forced her to reveal where the safe was. Money and jewellery to the value of five thousand pounds were handed over by Miss Martin, who was then tied to a chair. The alarm was raised at midnight, when the friend with whom she had spent the evening telephoned and received no reply. →

➡

5. In a public lavatory, with the door locked, Felicia feels her way through the belongings in the heavier of her carrier bags, to the jersey in which she has secreted the greater part of her money. She has two pounds and seventy-three pence left in the purse in her handbag.

But the sleeves of the jersey are empty and, thinking she has made a mistake, she searches the other bag. Since it yields nothing either, she returns to the first one. In a panic she takes everything out of both, littering the floor of the cubicle, unfolding the navy-blue jersey and shaking out all the other clothes. The money is not there.

(*Source: Felicia's Journey* by William Trevor)

6. Capri is essentially a fairy tale, a dream lost in the extraordinary azure of an incredible sea, in the boundless panoramas that embrace other precious tesserae of that wonderful mosaic that is the Neapolitan and Salerno coast, between Capo Miseno and Amalfi. Everything that can be perceived by the senses finds its greatest elevation on this island; from the light, sublime complement and refined facets of colour that allow one to read, as in an open book, the endless wonders of the place; from the perfume of the flowers that constitutes another jewel of the island and the vegetation that is a mixture of Mediterranean aspects and more precisely tropical ones: from the strong salt-laden breezes of a sea that is the very life of the island; from the disturbing voice of silence, broken only by the piercing cry of the seagulls and the breaking of the waves on the steep and precipitous rocks; from the possibility of touching with one's own hands the ancient traces of an illustrious and fascinating history, together with numerous remains of a past that represents the most authentic cultural matrix of the place.

(*Source: Capri. Ediz. Inglese*)

PRACTICE PAPER

TIGER MOTHER

(The full text appears in the Evaluation chapter, pages 60–61.)

Questions

1. Read again lines 1–10.
   a) Look at the opening sentence of the paragraph. Explain in your own words what it is that 'Chinese parents understand' that is key to their children's educational success. **(2 marks)**
   b) Summarise briefly the stages of the 'virtuous circle' by which Chinese children become very willing to study. **(5 marks)**
   c) Analyse how any one feature of the writer's language in lines 1–10 helps convey her meaning effectively. You could refer in your answer to a feature such as sentence structure, word choice, imagery, contrast, tone… **(2 marks)**
2. Read again lines 11–24.
   Explain how the two anecdotes described in lines 11–19 illustrate the different attitudes to parenting outlined in lines 20–24. **(4 marks)**
3. Explain the function of lines 25–26 in the structure of the writer's argument. **(2 marks)**
4. Read again lines 27–57.
   a) Identify the **three** differences described in these lines between Chinese and Western attitudes to parenting. You should use your own words as far as possible. **(3 marks)**
   b) By referring to at least two features of language in lines 27–57 analyse how the writer conveys the Chinese attitude to parenting. You should refer in your answer to such features as sentence structure, word choice, imagery, contrast, tone… **(4 marks)**

(There is advice on tackling questions 5 and 6 on pages 58–65.)

5. Evaluate the effectiveness of the final paragraph as a conclusion to the passage as a whole. **(3 marks)**

Question on both passages

6. Both passages look at the topic of bringing up children. Identify key areas where Jemima Lewis agrees or disagrees with Amy Chua.
   You may answer this question in continuous prose or in a series of developed bullet points. **(5 marks)**

Total: 30 marks

GLOSSARY OF TERMS

alliteration: a figure of speech in which there is repetition of initial and sometimes internal consonant sounds in a phrase, e.g. 'steely stare'.

ambiguity: language capable of being understood in more than one way (adjective is '**ambiguous**').

anecdote: a small story, often personal, included to illustrate an idea in a larger piece of work.

anti-climax: a sudden falling off at the end of a list that builds up in rank or significance; a sudden relaxation of tension.

antithesis: a sentence structure arranged symmetrically to present ideas as a balanced contrast.

antonym: a word meaning the opposite of another word.

aphorism: a short, pithy, sometimes cryptic saying (adjective is '**aphoristic**').

archaic: an old fashioned word or expression, e.g. 'thou' for 'you'.

atmosphere: the creation of mood, often through references to the senses, e.g. darkness suggests mystery or evil.

circumlocution: the roundabout expression of an idea, using more words than necessary.

climax: the culminating point in a list of things that builds in significance; the peak of tension.

colloquialism: the language of everyday speech. Includes abbreviations and contractions like 'can't', or informal expressions such as 'kid' instead of 'child'; interjections such as 'well', 'of course', 'you see'.

comparative: the form of an adjective indicating greater or lesser degree (comparing two things), e.g. 'younger', 'older'.

connotation: the associations of a word, or something associated with it, e.g. the colour white is associated with purity and innocence.

context: the immediate surroundings of a word or phrase; or the precise place in which it is used.

denotation: the literal meaning of a word.

dialect: the type of language used in a geographical area, e.g. 'lassie' is Scots for 'girl', 'bonnie' for 'pretty', 'burn' for 'stream'. (Note: dialect is *not* slang.)

diction: word choice; words selected by a poet or writer.

emotive: language that expresses the writer's emotions and aims to arouse emotion in the reader.

euphemism: a gentler way of expressing something unpleasant, e.g. 'passed away' rather than 'died'.

euphony: pleasant-sounding language (adjective is '**euphonious**').

evaluation: assessment of the effectiveness of writing.

expression: 'an expression' means a word or, more usually, a phrase; otherwise 'expression' means style of writing.

extended metaphor: see *metaphor*.

figurative language: an alternative word for metaphor; contrasts with literal (actual) meaning.

figure of speech: a general term for language techniques such as simile, metaphor, hyperbole, alliteration, oxymoron, irony, etc.

first person: using 'I', 'we', 'me', 'us' instead of 'he', 'they', etc.

hyperbole: exaggeration for dramatic or humorous effect.

illustration: a detailed example or a small story that acts as an example.

image: an unlike thing that something is compared to, which will have one or more points of similarity, e.g. in the expression 'the soldier was as brave as a lion', the image is 'lion', a fierce animal.

imagery: images used in similes and metaphors.

inversion: word order that places the verb before the subject or otherwise 'inverts' the usual word order of a sentence. This places emphasis on the word that is out of order, e.g. 'Down she went.'

irony: a form of mockery achieved by saying the opposite of what is really meant, or where the surface meaning differs from the underlying one, which is implied; adjective is **ironic** or **ironical**, meaning mocking or sarcastic.

jargon: technical language or language that is used by specialists of some kind; used critically to imply excessive or unintelligible use of such language.

juxtaposition: placing one thing beside another to create an effect, such as contrast.

link: a sentence (or sentences) that refers both to the idea just discussed and introduces the next one; any joining device in an argument, such as a conjunction.

litotes: understatement, especially by using a negative of the opposite, e.g. 'not bad'.

metaphor: a comparison where one thing is said to *be* another; a comparison without using 'like' or 'as'. An **extended metaphor** is a series of images in which the same comparison is sustained.

minor sentence: a sentence in which the verb is omitted, as understood.

monosyllable: a word of one syllable.

mood: the emotional feeling created in a piece of writing, e.g. anger, admiration.

onomatopoeia: a figure of speech in which the sound of a word imitates its sense, e.g. 'clip-clop'.

oxymoron: a figure of speech containing an apparent contradiction, e.g. 'sweet sorrow'.

paradox: an apparent contradiction of ideas, e.g. 'You must be cruel to be kind.'

parenthesis: a word, phrase or sentence inserted into a sentence, giving extra information.

personal: writing that refers to the writer's own experience and feelings, often in the first person; the personality of the writer will be clearly evident. (In the case of **impersonal writing**, the opposite will apply.)

personification: an inanimate object is spoken of as if it is alive or has a mind of its own.

polysyllable: a word with many syllables

register: a form of language used in restricted circumstances, e.g. legal language, medical terminology.

rhetoric: the language of formal speech, aiming to inspire/persuade/impress.

rhetorical question: a question that does not expect an answer, as the answer is assumed or seems obvious.

second person: the use of pronoun 'you' (both singular and plural).

sentence structure: types of sentence (statement, question, command, exclamation and minor sentence); word order, and the arrangement of phrases and clauses within a sentence.

simile: a figure of speech comparing two basically unlike things using 'like' or 'as'.

slang: a colloquial expression that is unacceptable in formal language, e.g. 'clobber'. Slang is often particular to an age group or period of time.

structure: the development of ideas in an argument or stages in a story.

superlative: the form of adjective indicating the highest degree, used in comparing three or more things, e.g. 'best', 'worst'.

synonym: a word meaning the same as another word.

syntax: the arrangement of words and phrases in a sentence.

tense: the form of a verb that indicates time of an action, e.g. past, present.

third person: the use of 'he', 'she', 'it' or 'they', as opposed to 'I' or 'we' (first person), or 'you' (second person).

tone: the expression of the writer's feelings or attitude to his subject, e.g. humorous, sarcastic.

understatement: expressing something as less than it is, or in a notably restrained way.

word choice: the writer's preference of certain words over others that have similar meanings.

ACKNOWLEDGEMENTS

The Publishers would like to thank the following for permission to reproduce copyright material:

Extracts from the article by Jessica Aldred, Copyright Guardian News & Media Ltd 2008;

Extract from the article by Bjørn Lomborg © Telegraph Media Group Limited 2013/2014;

The article by Cristina Odone, is abridged from the *Daily Telegraph* © Telegraph Media Group Limited 2013/2014;

Article by Michael Deacon, reproduced with permission of the *Daily Telegraph* © Telegraph Media Group Limited 2013/2014;

Extracts from articles by Jemima Lewis, reproduced by permission of the *Daily Telegraph* © Telegraph Media Group Limited 2013/2014;

The article by Craig Brown is adapted from the *Daily Mail* (13th February 2014);

Article by Andrew Malone, adapted from the *Daily Mail* (25th January 2014);

Speech given by Hillary Clinton for the 600th anniversary of St Andrews University, published by St Andrews University (www.st-andrews.ac.uk) on 13th September 2013;

Article by Angela Epstein, adapted from the *Daily Mail* (20th March 2008);

Article by Roger Lewis, published in the *Daily Mail* on 23rd January 2014;

Extract from the letters page appeared in the *Daily Mail* on 26th March 2014;

The article by Graeme Macpherson is reproduced with the permission of *The Herald* and *Sunday Herald* © Newsquest (Herald and Times) Ltd;

The article by Nick Foulkes is reproduced with the permission of the *Daily Telegraph* © Telegraph Media Group Limited 2013/2014;

Article by Jim McBeth, published in the *Daily Mail* (23rd December 2013);

The article by Ellen E. Jones is reproduced by permission of the *Independent*;

The article by Tom Chivers is reproduced by permission of the *Daily Telegraph* © Telegraph Media Group Limited 2013/2014;

The article by David Adam, published by the *Guardian*, copyright Guardian News & Media Ltd 2003;

Article by Sarah Vine, published in the *Daily Mail* (3rd December 2013);

The article by Grant Feller is reproduced by permission of GF-Media;

Article by A. A. Gill, adapted from the *Sunday Times Magazine* (29th March 2009);

Article by Lonnette Harrell, adapted from the *Yahoo Contributor Network* (voices.yahoo.com);

The article by Alan Taylor is reproduced with the permission of *The Herald* and *Sunday Herald* © Newsquest (Herald and Times) Ltd;

Article by Susan Swarbrick is reproduced with the permission of *The Herald* and *Sunday Herald* © Newsquest (Herald and Times) Ltd;

The article by Quentin Letts is adapted from the *Daily Mail* (27th February 2014);

Every effort has been made to trace all copyright holders, but if any have been inadvertently overlooked the Publishers will be pleased to make the necessary arrangments at the first opportunity.